Affective

Jacob's Ladder

Grades 4-5

Reading Comprehension Program Social-Emotional Intelligence

4   Short stories

Affective

Jacob's Ladder

Grades 4-5

Reading Comprehension Program
Social-Emotional Intelligence

Joyce VanTassel-Baska, Ed.D., &
Tamra Stambaugh, Ph.D.

PRUFROCK PRESS INC.
WACO, TEXAS

Prufrock Press Inc.
P.O. Box 8813
Waco, TX 76714-8813
Phone: (800) 998-2208
Fax: (800) 240-0333
http://www.prufrock.com

Table of Contents

Part I: Teachers' Guide to Affective Jacob's Ladder Reading Comprehension Program

Introduction

Affective Jacob's Ladder Reading Comprehension Program is a supplemental reading program that applies targeted readings and images from various genres of literature and visual media to link comprehension and analysis skills about affect. Using verbal and visual stimuli, the program invites students to engage in an inquiry process that moves from lower order to higher order levels of social-emotional awareness and thinking skills.

Starting with basic awareness and understanding, students learn to become aware of self and others, express emotion and needs, and create conditions and schema for maximizing potential for an optimal life. The ladders address both important skills for emotional well-being (risk-taking and managing stress) and desirable outcomes (acquiring emotional intelligence and developing excellence).

Rationale

Constructing meaning of the written word is one of the earliest tasks required of students in schools. This skill occupies the central place in the curriculum at the elementary level. Yet, approaches to teaching reading comprehension often are "skill and drill," using worksheets on low-level reading material. As a result, students frequently are unable to transfer these skills from exercise pages and apply them to new higher level reading material. This is especially the case when there is no attention to the affective and conative underpinnings to the process of reading. Several researchers have noted the need for motivation, persistence, and coping strategies that would entice students to move their learning to a higher level (McInerney & Ali, 2006; Pink, 2006; Zimmerman, 2000).

Affective Jacob's Ladder Reading Comprehension Program provides that affective bridge to encourage readers to develop skills that promote life skills as well as reading skills in areas like problem solving, developing empathy, and channeling emotion. Breaking down these skills into steps that can be internalized by the student further supports social-emotional learning (Collaborative for Academic, Social, and Emotional Learning [CASEL, 2017]; Gresham, 1995).

Research on emotional intelligence suggests that some skills such as emotional well-being, social effectiveness, social connectedness, and managerial effectiveness can be developed through a curriculum-based approach (Ciarrochi & Mayer, 2007), especially long-term interventions that are carefully implemented by a teacher who is sufficiently trained in the affective processes of open-ended questioning and inquiry. Quasi-experimental studies at upper elementary and middle school levels have found positive social, emotional, and academic outcomes when students are exposed to an emotional intelligence-based curriculum (Brackett, Rivers, Reyes, & Salovey, 2012; Maurer & Brackett, 2004). CASEL (2013) reported that a deliberate curricular focus on developing skills such as self-awareness (e.g., recognizing strengths, understanding emotions, belief in oneself), social awareness (e.g., empathy, perspective taking, appreciation of diversity), responsible decision making (e.g., identifying, analyzing, and reflecting on problems), developing relationships (e.g., communication and collaboration), and self-management (e.g., goal setting, organizational skills, managing stress) results in healthier and more productive lifestyles (see https://casel.org/impact for more information). A more recent meta-analysis of the effects of social-emotional curriculum on student behaviors and learning reported an 11-point gain in achievement scores when curriculum was deliberately taught and well-executed in the classroom (Durlak, Weissberg, Dymnicki, Taylor, & Schellinger, 2011).

Educators and researchers at all levels working with all abilities of students have begun to realize the importance and impact of the affective domain on learning in the classroom (CASEL, 2013; McCoach, Gable, & Madura, 2013). The basis for considering the importance of affective development of the gifted as the cornerstone of gifted curriculum comes from several sources and emerging theories in the field. Lines of research have included personal goal setting (Marisano & Shore, 2010), compassion (Hartsell, 2006), and coping mechanisms (Shaunessy & Suldo, 2010), just to name a few. Similarly, factors such as motivation and perseverance or task commitment impact an individual's talent development trajectory (Subotnik, Olszewski-Kubilius, & Worrell, 2011). Other less recent, but still important, research includes Moon's (2003) proposal of a theory of personal talent that suggests metacognitive control has a substantial impact on the capacity of a student to convert aptitudes into skills. Sternberg's (2006) idea that the individual's capacity to direct the talent development process in a proactive way is essential to optimal realization of positive outcomes. Older theories such as Gottfredson's (1996) career development model that stresses the use of ability indicators to create a trajectory or life path and Csikszentmihalyi's (1991) concept of flow are central to the affective emphases suggested in this text.

Therefore, the primary purpose of the *Affective Jacob's Ladder Reading Comprehension Program* is to combine English language arts (ELA) standards of textual analysis with social-emotional learning through the exploration of and identification with characters, themes, and situations within texts.

The Methodology of Using the *Affective Jacob's Ladder Reading Comprehension Program*

The use of books has long been lauded a stand-alone intervention in addressing the affective concerns of gifted learners but is magnified in effectiveness when paired with specific issues of the gifted population (Halsted, 2009). Bibliotherapy can be useful in helping these students explore issues of decision making (Friedman & Cataldo, 2002), identity development (Frank & McBee, 2003), emotional intelligence (Sullivan & Strang, 2002–2003), empathy (Ingram, 2003), social problems (Hébert & Kent, 1999), and multiculturalism (Ford, Tyson, Howard, & Harris, 2000), among others.

We also know that reading skills like comprehension are enhanced by instructional scaffolding, moving students from lower order to higher order thinking, using strategies and processes to help students analyze passages (Fisher & Frey, 2014; Peterson & Taylor, 2012). In addition, teachers who emphasize higher order thinking through questions and tasks, such as those at the higher rungs of each ladder, promote greater reading growth (Degener & Berne, 2016). The original *Jacob's Ladder Reading Comprehension Program* was written in response to teacher perceptions that students needed additional scaffolding to work consistently at higher levels of thinking in reading (see VanTassel-Baska & Stambaugh, 2006b).

In addition, the adoption of the Common Core State Standards (CCSS) in 2010, or state standards modeled on the CCSS, resulted in a new emphasis on the close reading of complex text. This involves making annotations, using text-dependent questions, and holding discussions about texts. Harvey and Goudvis (2007) have promoted the use of text coding and annotating as methods for students to deepen comprehension. In gifted education, the use of literary analysis and interpretation of single or multiple sources have been major tools for enhancing higher level thinking (VanTassel-Baska & Little, 2017).

In order to focus students' attention on specific elements of text in multiple readings, researchers have emphasized the need for teachers to provide text-dependent questions (Fisher & Frey, 2012; Lapp, Grant, Moss, & Johnson, 2013; Santori & Belfatti, 2017). Text-based discussion can facilitate reading comprehension by allowing students to construct their understanding of ideas in collaboration with their classmates (DeFrance & Fahrenbruck, 2015). Researchers have also noted the importance of discussions for enhancing student talk about texts for improving the comprehension of text (Duke, Pearson, Strachan, & Billman, 2011; Lawrence & Snow, 2011) and promoting thinking.

Many of the questions in *Jacob's Ladder* are text-dependent questions, although some ladders and questions are deliberately open-ended, as students are also encouraged to go beyond the text to make connections within and across other disciplines and to their own lives. Discussions may be conducted one-on-one, in dyads, small groups, or with the entire class.

The *Affective Jacob's Ladder Reading Comprehension Program* is a compilation of the instructional scaffolding and reading experiences necessary to aid students on their journey toward becoming strong readers, a goal that involves their emotional responses to the texts as well as their critical ones. This methodology deliberately moves students from simple to complex skills with grade-appropriate texts. Such a learning approach to skill development ensures that students can traverse easily from basic comprehension skills to higher level critical and creative reading skills, while using the same reading stimulus to navigate this transition.

The questions and tasks for each reading are open-ended, as this type of approach to responding to literature improves performance on comprehension tests (Wasik & Hindman, 2013). Progressing through the hierarchy of skills also requires students to re-read the text, thereby improving meta-comprehension accuracy (Hedin & Conderman, 2010). Students at all levels delight in discussing the meaning of a text and how to interpret it, as seen in our early studies of elementary students using the ladders. (See the Research Base section for more information.)

Audience

This book is suggested for gifted students in grades 4–5 who are already showing advanced levels of thinking and would benefit from discussing affective needs through textual and media-based prompts that support discussion. This book is also appropriate for use with typical learners who have strong textual analysis skills and who require more emphasis on affective development in their curriculum, including those who are twice-exceptional, students from poverty, and those from different cultural backgrounds (VanTassel-Baska & Stambaugh, 2006b). The reading selections include classic and contemporary literature and media that appeal to a wider audience than just the gifted. Many of the texts and resources were deliberately selected based on the inclusion of concepts that highlight experiences and struggles reported by gifted students. The ladder questions require students to have a basic understanding of a text before engaging in-depth with applications to their own affective development. It is easily argued that most students, whether identified as gifted or not, will benefit from affective development using processes outlined in this program, such as fear of failure, achieving goals, and peer relationships. However, not all students may be as concerned about these issues at as early of an age as they are dealt with in this book, nor in the same ways. Teachers can use their own discernment and understanding of their students to decide whether or not questions and textual prompts need to be modified for use with an entire group of students.

Research Base for the Jacob's Ladder Program

A quasi-experimental study was conducted using the *Jacob's Ladder Reading Comprehension Program* as a supplementary resource for grade 3–5 students in Title I schools. After receiving professional development, teachers were instructed to implement the *Jacob's Ladder* curriculum in addition to their basal reading series and guided reading groups.

Findings from this study ($N = 495$) suggested that, when compared to students who used the basal reader only, those students who were exposed to the *Jacob's Ladder* curriculum showed significant gains in reading comprehension and critical thinking. Likewise, students who used the curriculum showed significant and important growth on curriculum-based assessments that included determining implications and consequences, making inferences, outlining themes and generalizations, and applying creative synthesis. Students also reported greater interest in reading and suggested that the curriculum made them "think harder." Teachers reported more in-depth student discussion and personal growth in the ability to ask open-ended questions in reading (Stambaugh, 2007). Thus, the evidence suggests that the program is effective in enhancing basic and advanced reading skills in a context of student discussion of interesting texts.

Follow-up visitations to classrooms using the Jacob's Ladder materials demonstrate the effectiveness of the use of structured questions and activities to promote growth in gifted learners. Piloting of affective emphases appear promising when used in tandem with the cognitive materials already available. In addition, the theoretical frameworks for social-emotional learning also support the individual ladder development and focus.

Organization of the Material

Tasks are organized into eight skill ladders, E–L. Each ladder focuses on a different concept essential to affective growth and development. Underlying each ladder concept is a set of challenging skills that may be practiced in order to attain competence in the affective concept. Students "climb" each ladder by answering lower level questions before moving to higher level questions (or rungs) at the top of each ladder. Questions may also be used with activities to enhance deeper understanding of the concept. Many of the ladder frameworks are based on a theory of affective development found useful in working with gifted learners (e.g., the theory of positive psychology developed by Seligman & Csikszentmihalyi, 2014). Others are designed around types of intelligence in the affective realm, such as Mayer and Salovey's (1995) model of emotional intelligence or Goleman (1995) and Gardner's (2011) ideas of interpersonal and intrapersonal intelligence. The theories around conative constructs such as motivation, resilience, and persistence are also used as a basis for some of the ladders (see Dweck, 2006; Seligman & Csikszentmihalyi, 2014). Counseling theories that employ cognitive-behavioral techniques were also consulted (see Ellis, 1997).

Table 1 provides a visual representation of the eight ladders and corresponding objectives for each ladder and rung. A description of each of the eight ladders is also included in the narrative that follows.

TABLE 1
A List of Affective Ladders With Corresponding Student Objectives

Ladder E
Emotional Intelligence

Using Emotion

Discuss how one might channel emotions into a creative outlet and use emotions to create change or for a specific purpose or goal through literary texts or situations.

Expressing Emotion

Explain how emotions are conveyed through the use of literary elements in a text and convey one's own emotions in positive ways.

Understanding Emotion

Identify and understand different emotions and emotional language used to convey a message.

Ladder F
Coping With Adversity and Challenge

Facing Adversity and Challenges

Create or articulate solutions and discuss implications for facing adverse situations and challenges in a productive way.

Analyzing Adverse Situations and Conditions

Explain how adverse situations in self and others contributes to varying conditions and outcomes.

Recognizing Adversity and Challenge

Recognize adversity and challenge expressed in fictional and real-life texts and situations; explain how these challenges affect the individuals involved.

Ladder G
Risk-Taking

Engaging in Productive Risk-Taking

Design or explain a plan for productively engaging in healthy risks that promote one's achievement.

Considering Multiple Perspectives

Articulate, seek, or review multiple perspectives, ideas, or situations and weigh the outcomes.

Identifying and Calculating Risks

Identify potential risks in a situation and discuss the potential cause and effects of such risk on one's situation or outcome.

Ladder H
Developing Identity

Actualizing Potential to Advance a Goal

Create unique ideas, plans, and products that show an understanding of one's identity and how that identity allows for goal attainment.

Understanding Roles and Affiliations

Discuss how one's role and affiliation (or perception of his or her role/affiliation) supports or inhibits his or her personal growth.

Knowing Oneself

Explain fictional and individual characteristics and traits and assess the strengths and weaknesses of each as part of recognizing one's identity or how identity is crafted.

TABLE 1, Continued.

Ladder I Developing Empathy	Ladder J Stress Management	Ladder K Achievement Motivation	Ladder L Developing Talent and Excellence
Collaborating With Others	**Creating a Plan for Management**	**Reflecting on Patterns of Achievement**	**Demonstrating High-Level Performance in a Given Area**
Design collaboration plans or explain effective ways to collaborate or interact with others to achieve a specific purpose or goal.	Create a plan for managing stressors that includes specific criteria and outcomes or critique the effectiveness of one's plan for managing stress.	Develop attainable goals for long-term learning; synthesize patterns of achievement in oneself and others.	Create a new product, idea, or plan for developing one's strengths and attaining goals.
Communicating and Responding to Others	**Applying Stress Control Techniques**	**Assessing Strengths and Interests**	**Applying Learning to Practice**
Communicate effectively in a variety of ways and in response to one's needs; consider others' ideas and perspectives as part of a communication plan.	Apply healthy ways to manage stress to various situations, scenarios, or contexts.	Explain how the use of one's strengths and interests contributes to one's achievement.	Explain how to use or create opportunities and develop strengths to acquire knowledge; practice healthy habits for success and meeting one's own goals.
Understanding Others' Needs and Values	**Identifying Conditions/ Situations That Cause Stress**	**Identifying Barriers to Achievement**	**Recognizing Internal and External Factors That Promote Talent Development**
Identify and explain the needs of others through perspectives other than one's own; put oneself in another's situation and discuss ideas from that perspective.	Identify and explain conditions that cause stress in others and oneself.	Identify and explain personal and external barriers to achievement.	Identify and explain personal and external factors that impede or promote talent development, including what is and is not in one's control.

Ladder E: Emotional Intelligence

The goal of Ladder E is to help students develop skills in using their emotional intelligence in order to regulate and modulate behavior with respect to learning. It moves from students' understanding of emotion in self and others, to expressing emotion, to channeling emotion for cognitive ends. Adapted from the work of Mayer and Salovey (1995) on emotional intelligence, the rungs progress through certain aspects of their framework. The rungs are as follows:

- **Ladder E, Rung 1, Understanding Emotion:** The lowest rung on Ladder E is understanding emotion in oneself and others. This requires students to identify emotions in characters and relate them to their own lives. For example, what feelings does the main character portray throughout the story? How would you compare his temperament to yours? It also requires them to recognize emotional situations and pinpoint the nature of the emotions involved and what is causing them. Many of the poetry and visual media selections are employed to engage students in the use of this ladder.

- **Ladder E, Rung 2, Expressing Emotion:** The middle rung on Ladder E, expressing emotion, asks students to express emotion in response to their reading of various selections. For example, the main character seems to worry too much. Is worry ever beneficial? Why or why not? As part of the expression of emotion, it is important that students begin to recognize appropriate and inappropriate expressions. Within the context of a reading curriculum, students may be asked to express their own emotions about a particular situation, event, or character's actions in self-selected formats, including poetry or prose. Teachers may want to substitute kinesthetic responses in the form of dance or skits that demonstrate an emotional reaction to the selections. Students may also be asked to analyze how other characters expressed emotions in ways that were positive or negative.

- **Ladder E, Rung 3, Using Emotion:** The highest rung on Ladder E, using emotion, encourages students to begin regulating emotion for specific purposes or goals. For example, how does worry impact your life? What steps can you take to minimize worry? Write a personal action plan or determine how emotions can help/hinder students reaching goals. In application to poetry, prose, and nonfiction, students need to demonstrate a clear understanding of how to use emotion effectively for accomplishing specific ends, whether through giving a speech or writing a passionate letter in defense of an idea. The deliberate incorporation of emotion coupled with evidence and achieving a goal in one's communication is stressed.

Note. In addition to the rung categories as described above, at times this ladder may also be used to help students convey their own emotions and evoke emotion in readers by deliberately analyzing and applying literary techniques. In these instances, E1 focuses on identifying how words or literary techniques (i.e., figurative language, alliteration, structure) were used to evoke feelings or recognizing words and features within a text that promote feelings. E2 focuses on how the author uses these words in context with other techniques to convey a message or evoke emotional appeals, while E3 encourages students to show understanding by applying literary techniques to their own work with a specific purpose or goal.

Ladder F: Coping With Adversity and Challenge

The goal of Ladder F is to move students from recognizing adversity and challenges they (or others) are facing to analyzing the conditions that have created the challenge, and finally to resolving the situation through reframing and problem solving. The following ladder provides the structure for students to apply positive coping mechanisms, based on the work of Vaillant (1992), cognitive behavioral therapy by Beck (1979), the work of Dai and Speerschneider (2012), and Seligman, Rashid, and Parks' (2006) work in positive psychology.

- **Ladder F, Rung 1, Recognizing Adversity and Challenge:** The lowest rung on Ladder F requires students to recognize and confront their understanding of adverse and challenging situations and contexts that they encounter in the text or in viewing material they accessed. They must identify the special challenges faced by characters (e.g., What barriers is the character encountering in life? What is causing that barrier to be a problem?), and then be able to transfer that understanding to their own lives.

- **Ladder F, Rung 2, Analyzing Adverse Situations and Conditions:** Beyond recognition of adverse conditions, students must break down the components of challenge in order to understand them more deeply. For example, what are the factors that affected Hamlet's decision making about killing his uncle? How did they interact to cause his inaction? By so doing, students can begin to better understand the complexity of adversity in all of its manifestations.

- **Ladder F, Rung 3, Facing Adversity and Challenges:** Reaching a resolution from addressing challenges and coping with adversity represents the highest level of the work in this ladder. Students restate and review the challenges in a way that allows them to identify how to overcome barriers and to design a workable plan of action, or to know when it might be time to give up on an idea and move to a different solution or decision.

Ladder G: Risk-Taking

The goal of Ladder G is to promote more open-ended thinking, feeling, and behavior in gifted students when they approach reading material and other intellectual situations and contexts in their own life. It is critical that they assess the nature and extent of the risk they may be taking, feel comfortable expressing their own opinions, even when they conflict with the stated opinions of others, and be able to create their own stance or statement about a stimulus, such as a text, a film, or media event. The following ladder promotes the development of more open-ended behavior in the learner as suggested by research (Bandura, 1986; Beghetto, 2010; Brackett et al., 2012):

- **Ladder G, Rung 1, Identifying and Calculating Risks:** Risk, in the intellectual sense, refers to being open to experience, to challenge the status quo when appropriate, and to voice one's own views. Yet students must also come to weigh the consequences of speaking out against prevailing opinion and to prepare arguments to support their viewpoints. They need to be comfortable with ambiguity and aware of the risks involved, as well as their own strengths and weaknesses.

- **Ladder G, Rung 2, Considering Multiple Perspectives:** Students at the second rung of this ladder learn to express themselves in an articulate way, both orally and in writing, in order to communicate perspectives. They frame opinions based on hearing or reading what others have said about an issue and filter these opinions through their own thinking and feeling mechanisms. They also learn that the most important questions have no right answers and therefore require an open mind to hear and discuss multiple perspectives, and that the most important issues are never solved but only resolved at a particular point in time, due to deadlines and other mandatory requirements for closure (see Paul, 1992).

- **Ladder G, Rung 3, Engaging in Productive Risk-Taking:** At the highest rung of the ladder on risk-taking, students encounter the challenge of creating an alternative stance and applying calculated risks to their decision. They must decide on their own stance, decision, or perspective and then develop a product or action that represents it, such as a speech, a written statement, or an organized plan of action.

Ladder H: Developing Identity

The goal of Ladder H is to enhance identity development in students, helping them develop personal awareness through reflective assessment of strengths and weaknesses, as well as their affiliations and own personal beliefs. Students also need to develop relationships with others to understand how they are perceived and to reflect on their own behavior as a result of those interactions that may shape their own identity. Finally, students need to move toward actualizing behavior that reflects their ability to be goal-directed in an independent way that encourages fulfillment of their own potential and recognition of and comfort with who they are and what they want. The following ladder promotes such development, supported by the work of Csikszentmihalyi (1991, 1996), Maslow (1961), O'Connor and Rosenblood (1996), and Erikson (1994).

- **Ladder H, Rung 1, Knowing Oneself:** At the lowest ladder on intrapersonal development, students encounter text and visual media that requires them to reflect on their own beliefs, values, interests, and predilections. They encounter the need to assess their strengths and weaknesses for purposes of personal growth.

- **Ladder H, Rung 2, Understanding Roles and Affiliations:** Just as the emphasis of the first rung of the ladder is on introspection, the second rung requires students to consider how to develop relationships with others by examining outward behavior. They examine a character's internal and external development and affiliations (or lack thereof) that inform his identity. They also analyze the interactions of characters with each other, relating it to their own lives and situations.

- **Ladder H, Rung 3, Actualizing Potential to Advance a Goal:** At the highest rung of the ladder, students demonstrate how they would take charge of a situation to promote and defend an idea based on their own personal ideas, affiliations, research, feelings, or goals. The development of a plan and its execution is necessary to articulate the level of understanding that students may gain through traversing to this level of the ladder.

Ladder I: Developing Empathy

The development of empathy for others is seen by many as a key skill set that gifted students need, although many of these students already have well-developed abilities in this area. In order to develop this quality, however, students need to understand the needs and values of others, noting the similarities and differences to their own. They then need to develop oral and written responses to others, based on that understanding. Finally, students will develop the skills of collaboration, where they are working in a goal-directed atmosphere on verbal and nonverbal stimuli. Based on the work of Pinker (2011), Goleman (1995), Bar-On (2006), and others, the following rungs promote the development of such skills:

- **Ladder I, Rung 1, Understanding Others' Needs and Values:** At this first rung of this ladder, students consider the importance of understanding the needs and values of others, being able to articulate that understanding in relationship to their own.

- **Ladder I, Rung 2, Communicating and Responding to Others:** The second rung of this ladder requires students to respond to the needs of others, based on an analysis of needs. Students need to discern how best to respond and how to apply resources on behalf of other people. They mobilize their abilities to communicate for others in both oral and written form, such as writing an argument to provide power to Puerto Rico as quickly as possible post Tropical Storm Maria or debating the positive benefits of the Clean Air Act as essential to the children of American society.

- **Ladder I, Rung 3, Collaborating With Others:** At the highest rung of the ladder on empathy, students encounter the complex challenges of working with others toward a common goal, demonstrating both leadership and followership capacities. They use their skills of working with others to bring a project to fruition through team efforts, acknowledging different expertise and perspectives to support particular aspects of the work.

Ladder J: Stress Management

The goal of Ladder J relates to the need for students to develop mechanisms for monitoring and reducing their own stress. In order to do that, they need to be able to identify the situation and conditions that create fears of success and failure, be able to apply control techniques that can be used to reduce or remove the stressful context, and finally, be able to create a system for managing these fears. Readings about characters and real people who have encountered fear are used to elicit personal responses from students for use in discussion and writing. Consistent with research on depression and positive psychology (see Seligman et al., 2006), Glasser's choice theory, and internal locus of control (see Glasser, 1999; Rotter, 1966), the following ladder defines a pathway for such affective development.

- **Ladder J, Rung 1, Identifying Conditions/Situations That Cause Stress:** At the first rung of the ladder on stress management, students must encounter what makes life stressful with respect to the conditions and contexts where it occurs. What is the role of fear? What is the role of external pressure? How do others cause us to react against our best interests? These questions and others are considered as students read and react to textual material.

- **Ladder J, Rung 2, Applying Stress Control Techniques:** In the second rung of the ladder, students begin to understand how to control the demands of people and events in their lives, practicing the skills of saying no, of setting limits on time and resources, and considering ways to conquer fear through modeling on what others have done. They also understand what is within their power to control and what is not. For example, how can I manage my long-term project expectations over a 6-week period outside of school? What will I need to balance in order to study sufficiently for my upcoming test?

- **Ladder J, Rung 3, Creating a Plan for Management:** At the top rung of this ladder, students begin to develop a system of management for stress that engages them in recognizing that they have choices within their control and may develop criteria for use in situations they encounter in reading and in real life. What might characters do to reduce the stress in their lives? How might I handle my various commitments of school, home, and community within the time frame available? How do I ensure that I get enough sleep each night to be effective the next day? What choices are within my control? What power do I have over situations? These questions are asked by students as they consider ways to protect their time and resources and make good choices that support healthy decision making and lifestyles.

Ladder K: Achievement Motivation

The goal of Ladder K is to help students recognize both achievement and underachievement patterns in themselves and others. It is also to help them assess what internal and external barriers may be keeping them from wanting to perform or complete a task. Underachievement may be caused by a variety of factors. Influenced by the work of Bandura and Dweck (1985) and McClelland, Atkinson, Clark, and Lowell (1953), students are encouraged to acknowledge and assess barriers that keep them from achieving, seek support systems to help them set realistic goals and realize small successes, and assess and monitor their success by playing to their strengths, continually improving, and setting longer term goals.

- **Ladder K, Rung 1, Identifying Barriers to Achievement:** The first rung of the ladder asks students to assess what barriers hinder motivation and achievement. They are encouraged to consider environmental conditions, beliefs, values, skill sets, perceptions, and interests to determine the underlying cause for not performing. For example, if a student is not turning in homework, why not? Do students feel they have the skills to do the work? Are the assignments worth their time and effort or are they too easy or too hard? Is the environment conducive to achievement? Awareness of the underlying problem for underachieving is the first step toward changing the course of behavior.

- **Ladder K, Rung 2, Assessing Strengths and Interests:** Once students have determined the underlying causes of underachievement, they can capitalize on assets within themselves and their environment to achieve goals. They can apply their own interests and strengths to the task and solicit the help of others to support their goals. This can include rewards and celebrations of small successes and other reinforcements that encourage desired behaviors and an ongoing drive to succeed.

- **Ladder K, Rung 3, Reflecting on Patterns of Achievement:** The highest rung of the ladder encourages students to continue on a path toward achievement, moving away from rewards and short-term successes, and into longer term goal setting and the acceptance of challenges that continue to provide tasks that will require motivation to succeed.

Ladder L: Developing Talent and Excellence

The goal of Ladder L is to persuade gifted learners to adopt a model of personal excellence where learning is the goal, not performance per se, while reducing tendencies that inhibit their achievement (VanTassel-Baska, MacIntosh, & Kearney, 2015). In order to develop this approach, students first need to understand their own values and beliefs and recognize the source of their need to earn all As or to turn in perfect homework papers. They need to focus on learning and setting personal bests as goals for excellence, not perfection. Next, they need to recognize and apply the learning skills that will improve long-term performance, such as practice and persistence, given structured feedback from a teacher. Lastly, they need to be able to set goals and criteria for addressing them that would move them to a higher level of performance in an area of learning. Based on the work of Dweck (2006) and Sternberg (2006), the following ladder reflects a way to develop personal excellence:

- **Ladder L, Rung 1, Recognizing Internal and External Factors That Promote Talent Development:** The first rung of the ladder on developing personal excellence requires students to identify what they believe about themselves as an individual and a learner. This means being honest about their strengths, limitations, and skill sets, with the understanding that they can do something to improve these skills.

- **Ladder L, Rung 2, Applying Learning to Practice:** The second rung of the ladder asks students to engage in using learning skills rather than performance skills in addressing academic challenges they face. Students may be asked to consider difficult problems that cannot be solved, but must be addressed; learning outcomes that require more time than they have; and situations that require applied intelligence and effort.

- **Ladder L, Rung 3, Demonstrating High-Level Performance in a Given Area:** The highest rung of this ladder asks students to consider their own goals for personal excellence and the criteria they might use to create them. What are the factors necessary to make progress on a project? How might I apply myself to improve key skills? What areas of growth will I want to see in myself at the end of the year? What are my goals for learning in my talent area? These questions and more are central to student considerations of developing excellence.

Process Skills

Along with the eight main goals addressed by each ladder, a ninth goal focusing on process skills is incorporated in the *Affective Jacob's Ladder* curriculum. The aim of this goal is to promote learning through interaction and discussion of reading material in the classroom. After completing the ladders and following guidelines for discussion and teacher feedback, students will be able to:

- articulate their understanding of a reading passage, using emotional response and textual support;

- engage in reflection about the feeling and meaning of a selection;

- connect passages and meaning to their own life circumstances or others around them; and

- discuss varied ideas about the intention of a passage, both orally and in writing.

These process skills have been found to be consonant with several of the reading skills emphasized in national and state standards.

Reading Genres and Selections

The reading selections in *Affective Jacob's Ladder Reading Comprehension Program* include multiple genres of literature and visual media: short stories, songs, poetry, nonfiction selections, and biographies. Each reading has been selected based on key conceptual understandings, appropriate and engaging content, and vividness of grade-appropriate illustrations and supports, although this particular set of ladders would be appropriate for many students in the targeted grade levels.

Affective Jacob's Ladder Reading Comprehension Program, Grades 4–5 consists of 24 selections for students to read, view, and/or discuss. The readings and ladder exercises are designed to move students forward in their understanding of language, reading comprehension, self-awareness, and textual analysis. The vocabulary in each reading is generally grade-level appropriate; however, when new or unfamiliar words are encountered, they should be covered in class before the readings and ladders are assigned.

The short stories and poetry readings with corresponding ladder sets are delineated in Part II. Table 2 outlines all *Affective Jacob's Ladder Reading Comprehension Program, Grades 4–5* readings by genre.

TABLE 2
Affective Jacob's Ladder Grades 4–5 Selections by Genre

Short Stories and Media	Poetry	Biographies
The Man, the Boy, and the Donkey by Aesop	*Success Is Counted Sweeter* by Emily Dickinson	Engineers: Failure and Success
Wonder Trailer	*Mending* by Hazel Hall	The Buddy Bench
Music by Arya Okten	*The Fool's Song* by William Carlos Williams	*A Literary Lesson on Making Mistakes* by Madeleine Deisen
Eleven by Sandra Cisneros	*Casey at the Bat* by Ernest Lawrence Thayer	*Girls in STEM* by Karishma Muthukumar
The Leaping Match by Hans Christian Andersen	*A Lazy Day* by Paul Laurence Dunbar	Otis Boykin
Geri's Game written and directed by Jan Pinkava	*Winter Branches* by Margaret Widdemer	Stress Is Not the Enemy
The Four Crafts-Men by Jacob Grimm and Wilhelm Grimm	*From a Bridge Car* by Elias Lieberman	Jacqueline Woodson
Piper written and directed by Alan Barillaro		Lou Gehrig Farewell Speech
		A Happy Life

Implementation Considerations

Teachers need to consider certain issues when implementing the *Affective Jacob's Ladder Reading Comprehension Program* curriculum. Because modeling, coaching, and feedback appear to enhance student growth in reading and writing (Pressley et al., 2001; Taylor, Peterson, Pearson, & Rodriguez, 2002), it is recommended that teachers review how to complete the task ladders with the entire class at least once, outlining expectations and record-keeping tasks, as well as modeling the process prior to assigning small-group or independent work. As students gain more confidence in the curriculum, teachers should allow more independent work coupled with small-group or paired discussion, and then whole-group sharing with teacher feedback. The material *is not* intended to be used as worksheets or individual tasks, but rather for the facilitation of ongoing discussion, thinking, and self-awareness. High-ability learners often learn to read holistically and ahead of age peers (Little, 2017), making the need for teacher judgment crucial in deciding on materials to use for advanced reading at these levels. Completing these activities in dyads or small groups will facilitate discussions that stress collaborative reasoning, thereby fostering greater engagement and higher level thinking (Chin, Anderson, & Waggoner, 2001; Pressley et al., 2001; Taylor et al., 2002).

The readings and accompanying ladder questions and activities also may be organized into a reading center in the classroom or utilized with reading groups during guided reading for those students who are independent readers. Teachers may also choose to read the selections aloud to students in advanced-level reading groups or to the entire class and solicit responses through methods like think-pair-share, whole-group class discussion, or small-group/individual assignments to be completed prior to engaging in a reading group.

Because this set of *Jacob's Ladder* readings focuses on self-awareness and some social-emotional aspects, encouraging more opportunities for text-to-self connections, it is important that the classroom environment is set up in a way that promotes a safe environment for sharing ideas. Students need to feel comfortable in sharing their feelings and experiences, as well as ideas about the readings. Some students may only feel comfortable discussing questions related to the text or the perspective of a character without sharing personal experiences or questions. Teachers need a plan in place to honor this.

This also means that teachers may need additional training regarding how to best facilitate ideas and when and how to redirect sensitive topics and find a more appropriate venue for some students to share or process their ideas. Familiarity with school policies about when to refer students for counseling allows for proactive support. Collaborative discussions in class with a school counselor could also aid in implementation. Students with serious reactions to the material should always be referred to the school counselor who then may determine intervention needs beyond the school. Although these caveats are included, it is important to note that the design and purpose of *The Affective Jacob's Ladder Reading Comprehension Program* is to help students become more self-aware and practice positive habits through a more complex text-to-self analysis.

Teacher Use of Inquiry

Beck and McKeown (1998) suggested that academic discourse in reading promotes textual understanding. They recommended guiding students through the text by showing them how to mark keywords in a text both on their own and as part of whole-group modeling. Knowing that teacher stance is critical to the process of reasoning and understanding, teachers are encouraged to help students use evidence from the text to justify responses, including turning back in the text to show where ideas were found. Teachers should also model metacognitive approaches by thinking aloud about how one may go about developing an idea or comment, providing annotations or background information as necessary and then synthesizing key ideas expressed during a discussion. This guidance will promote critical thinking when combined with the discourse of also asking targeted, open-ended questions to help students gain understanding for themselves, without being told what to think.

Sample follow-up questions and prompts such as those listed below can be used by the teacher and posted in the classroom to guide student discussion. These questions are a mixture of cognitive and affective stimuli to encourage a balance between thinking and feeling about a text.

- That's interesting; does anyone have a different idea?

- What in the story makes you say that?

- What feelings does the story or poem evoke in you? Why?

- What do you think the author means by . . . ?

- What do you think are the implications or consequences of . . . ?

- In the story I noticed that . . . How might that explain the character's motivation?

- I heard someone say that they thought the poem (story) was about . . . What do you think? Justify your answer from the events of the story.

- What keywords might be significant? Why?

- Why might we have so many different responses to this situation?

- What motivated the character to act in the way he or she did? Do you agree or disagree?

- What words convey emotion in the poem, do you think? How effective are they? What do they symbolize?

- I agree (or disagree) with . . . because . . .

- How does your experience or interpretation differ from . . . ?

- What other (steps, decisions, responses, or reactions) would be appropriate in this situation?

The process of inquiry and feedback, as led and modeled by the teacher is critical to the success of the program and student mastery of process skills. Teachers need to solicit multiple student responses and encourage dialogue about various perspectives and interpretations of a given text, requiring students to justify their answers with textual support and concrete examples (VanTassel-Baska & Stambaugh, 2006a, 2006b).

Grouping Students

Affective Jacob's Ladder Reading Comprehension Program may be used in a number of different grouping patterns. The program should be introduced initially as a whole-group activity directed by the teacher with appropriate open-ended questions, feedback, and monitoring. After students have examined each type of ladder with teacher guidance, they should be encouraged to use the program by writing ideas independently, sharing with a partner, and then discussing the findings with a group. The dyad approach provides maximum opportunities for student discussion of the readings and collaborative decisions about the answers to questions posed. One purpose of these materials is to provide readings and discussion platforms that may lead to improving social and emotional skills and self-awareness through textual analysis. Another purpose of the program is to solicit meaningful discussion of the text, which is best accomplished in small groups of students at similar reading levels (VanTassel-Baska & Little, 2017). Independent reading is less preferred for the purposes of collaborative exchange. However, many younger high-ability learners may prefer the independence and opportunity to talk with the teacher one-on-one or have small group-guided discussions. Research continues to support instructional grouping in reading as an important part of successful implementation of any program that involves gifted learners (Rogers, 2002; Steenbergen-Hu, Makel, & Olszewski-Kubilius, 2016).

Demonstrating Growth: Pre- and Postassessments and Student Products

The pre- and postassessments included in Appendix A were designed as a diagnostic-prescriptive approach to guide program implementation of *Affective Jacob's Ladder*. The pretest should be administered, scored, and then used to guide student instruction and the selection of readings based on student needs. Both the pre- and postassessment and rating scale are included in Appendix A.

In both the pre- and postassessments, students read a biography and respond to the three questions. Question 1 focuses on reading responses through summarizing the relationship between emotion and literary techniques. Question 2 assesses students' knowledge of key themes and individual responses or motivations in dealing with a problem or situation through the interpretation or explanation, and Question 3 examines students' ability to make connections and inferences between the meaning of the text and their lives. Although self-awareness and social-emotional development are the focus of the readings and questions, scoring is based upon students' interpretation of the text, use of evidence to support ideas, and connections and awareness of the textual themes to real-world or personal situations.

Upon conclusion of the program or as a midpoint check, the postassessment may be administered to compare the preassessment results and to measure growth in students' responses. These pre-post results could be used as part of a student portfolio, to share in a parent-teacher conference, or as documentation of curriculum effectiveness and student progress.

Student Feedback and Record Keeping

Teachers will want to check student answers as ladder segments are completed and conduct an individual or small-group consultation to ensure that students understand why their answers may be effective or ineffective. Appendix A also includes a discussion checklist that teachers may use to analyze whether or not students understand key content through group or individual responses that may not be in writing. In order to analyze student responses and progress across the program, teachers need to monitor student performance, providing specific comments about student work to promote growth and understanding of content. As previously recommended, discussions that are more personal in nature need to be monitored and students may choose to opt out of sharing personal information or may need guidance in what and how much to share in a group setting versus privately, per school or state policies.

Record-keeping sheets for differentiation within the class are provided in Appendix B. On these forms, teachers record student progress on a 3-point scale: 2 (*applies skills very effectively*), 1 (*understands and applies skills*), or a 0 (*needs more practice with the given skill set*) across readings and ladder sets. These forms may be used as part of a diagnostic-prescriptive approach to selecting reading materials and ladders based on student understanding or the need for more practice. Teachers may select readings commensurate with key ladder skills needed by individual students and then flexibly group those students according to their levels of understanding of a particular ladder focus.

Grading

Grading the ladders and responses is at the teacher's discretion. Teachers should emphasize somewhat equally all rungs in graded activities. Lower rungs are typically part of a model for developing an affective skill and higher level activities and questions more likely may be found at the higher rungs of any given ladder. The top-rung questions and product suggestions may be used as a graded activity. Grades also could be given based on guided discussion after students are trained on appropriate ways to discuss literature. Additional prompts for grading are as follows:

- Explain how the central conflict of a text was resolved using literary techniques and appropriate or inappropriate social-emotional skills or processes.

- Explain how tone and mood were used to develop the theme of the story and evoke emotion of the reader.

- Create a symbol that exemplifies a particular person's response to overcoming adversity. Write two sentences to explain your symbol in relation to the text.

- In one word or phrase, what does this story mostly convey about developing excellence? Justify your answer using examples from the story. (Note that any skill or ladder purpose could be substitute for "developing excellence." For example, "what does this story mostly convey about overcoming adversity? Taking healthy risks? The relationship between hard work and luck?")

- Write a poem to express your emotions about something you feel strongly about, using the same literary techniques as modeled by the author.

As previously recommended, discussions that are more personal in nature need to be monitored. Students may opt out of sharing personal information or may need guidance about what and how much to share in a group setting versus privately, per school or state policies. Group norms should be established with examples and nonexamples for sharing provided. A school counselor can be invited to assist with establishing the process.

Time Allotment

Although the time needed to complete *Affective Jacob's Ladder Reading Comprehension Program* tasks will vary by student, most lessons should take students 15–30 minutes to read the selection aloud or with a partner (or to view the selection) and another 20–30 minutes to complete one ladder individually. More time is required for paired student and whole-group discussion of the questions or for specific creative synthesis tasks that involve more writing or researching. Teachers may wish to set aside 2 days each week for focusing on one *Affective Jacob's Ladder* reading and commensurate ladders, especially when introducing the program.

NAGC Program Standards and Alignment to *The Affective Jacob's Ladder Reading Comprehension Program*

The purpose of the NAGC Programming Standards is to provide a layer of support to schools so that they are aware of the characteristics of quality programs. The 36 student outcomes are organized within six Programming Standards: learning and development, assessment, curriculum planning and instruction, learning environments, programming, and professional development. (To download the standards, visit http://www.nagc.org/resources-publications/resources/national-standards-gifted-and-talented-education/pre-k-grade-12.) Standards 1, 3, and 4 provide strong connections to *Affective Jacob's Ladder*.

Standard 1 recognizes that students with gifts and talents have learning and developmental differences. The student outcomes encourage the students' ongoing self-understanding, awareness of their needs, and cognitive and affective growth in the school, home, and community.

Standard 3 emphasizes the importance of a teacher's knowledge and use of a core and specialized curriculum in challenging gifted and talented students. The standards stress talent development, instructional strategies, culturally relevant curriculum, and accessing appropriate resources to engage a variety of learners. Desired outcomes include students demonstrating growth commensurate with their aptitude, becoming competent in talent areas and as independent investigators, and developing knowledge and skills for being productive in a multicultural, diverse, and global society.

The creation of safe, inclusive, and culturally responsive learning environments is included as Standard 4. These environments provide the framework for a continuum of services that respond to an individual's gifts, talents, motivations, culture, and linguistic differences. Specific student outcomes include the development of self-awareness, self-advocacy, self-efficacy, confidence, motivation, resilience, independence, and curiosity. Students also learn how to develop positive peer relationships, social interactions, and interpersonal and technical communication skills with diverse individuals and across diverse groups. In their development of leadership skills, they also demonstrate personal and social responsibility.

Affective Jacob's Ladder Reading Comprehension Program addresses many of the elements of these three standards in the ladder sets of activities. There is a strong connection to the affective needs of gifted learners throughout the materials that stress intrapersonal and interpersonal skillsets. The material also focuses strongly on the development of communication skills that allow for affective development to occur, culminating in the development of leadership through the application of skills necessary to plan and organize one's own life and provide a model for others.

Common Core State Standards for English Language Arts

The Common Core State Standards are K–12 content standards, developed in math and language arts, to illustrate the curriculum emphases to develop in all students the skills and concepts needed for the 21st century. Adopted by the majority of states to date and used as a model by others, the standards are organized into key content strands and articulated across all years of schooling. The initiative has been state-based and collaboratively led through two consortia and coordinated by the National Governors Association (NGA) and the Council of Chief State School Officers (CCSSO). Designed by teachers, administrators, and content experts, the standards seek to prepare K–12 students for college and the workplace. National assessments, designed by two consortia, have been forged to judge student growth on the standards. To date, results have been sketchy and to some extent disappointing, with some states not reporting results publicly or indicating dissatisfaction with the results (NGA, 2013).

The standards in language arts are evidence-based, aligned with expectations for success in college and the workplace, and informed by the successes and failures of the current standards and international competition demands. They stress rigor, depth, clarity, and coherence, drawing from key national and international reports in mathematics and science. They provide a framework for curriculum development work currently being done by states and other agencies.

In addition to cognitive skills, the standards call for students to be able to collaborate with peers, to self-assess their own work, and to use innovative strategies to learning. These outcomes require the development of strong inter- and intrapersonal skills, and the application of emotional intelligence, all key features of the *Affective Jacob's Ladder Reading Comprehension Program*.

Affective Jacob's Ladder Reading Comprehension Program Alignment Approaches to Standards

Affective Jacob's Ladder Reading Comprehension Program exemplifies a model curriculum that addresses the Common Core State Standards in English language arts through several approaches including advanced readings, the use of higher level skills and product demands that address the CCSS emphases for argument and persuasion directly, the use of textual evidence, relationships between different textual elements, and a focus on concept/theme development that is mirrored in the new standards. Different from the other *Jacob's Ladder Reading Comprehension Program* books, the *Affective Jacob's Ladder* series promotes both textual analysis and social-emotional learning, although the emphasis remains on understanding texts and articulating ideas using appropriate evidence.

There are three major strategies the authors of the *Affective Jacob's Ladder Reading Comprehension Program* have used to accomplish the alignment to the Common Core State Standards.

First, *Affective Jacob's Ladder* provides pathways to advance the learning of the Common Core State Standards for gifted learners. Some of the standards address higher level skills and concepts that should receive focus throughout the years of schooling, such as a major emphasis on the skills of argument in language arts. However, there are also more discrete skills that may be clustered across grade levels and compressed around higher level skills and concepts for more efficient mastery by the gifted. The *Affective Jacob's Ladder Reading Comprehension Program* moves students from lower order understanding skills in affective areas to higher order use of affective skills to create products within the same set of activities, thus advancing their higher level learning in both cognitive and affective domains.

Secondly, the program provides differentiated task demands to address specific Common Core State Standards. Standards, such as the research standard in the Common Core State Standards for English Language Arts, lend themselves to differentiated interpretation by demonstrating what a typical learner might be able to do at a given stage of development versus what a gifted learner might be able to do. The differentiated examples in *Affective Jacob's Ladder* show greater complexity and creativity, using a more advanced curriculum base by combining textual elements and conceptual understandings with the understanding of oneself. Moving systematically to the more advanced levels of developing affective skills, gifted students may learn more quickly and deeply the integrated nature of cognitive understanding and affective supports.

Lastly, the *Affective Jacob's Ladder Reading Comprehension Program* features interdisciplinary product demands, based on the Common Core State Standards for English Language Arts. Because English language arts standards can be grouped together in application, much of the project work in *Affective Jacob's Ladder* connects to the Common Core State Standards and shows how multiple standards can be addressed across content areas. For example, speaking and listening, writing, and literary analysis standards may be met within one product demand as students are asked to write a new poem or story that applies various literary techniques to convey their own message and share it with an appropriate audience using effective methods to convey ideas. Students may also be asked to convey ideas and represent their ideas in tables, graphs, or other displays or to examine how the social context of a time period affects one's response to an event. This approach to interdisciplinary work across math, science, and language arts is a central part of the *Affective Jacob's Ladder* program at the elementary and middle school levels.

Conclusion

The *Affective Jacob's Ladder Reading Comprehension Program* presents a new opportunity for teachers of the gifted and others to provide their students a set of affective experiences that support their social-emotional learning through textual analysis. Organized around researched theories of human development in the affective arena, the program seeks to educate gifted and other students on the importance of other factors besides intelligence or deep knowledge of a content area in understanding and negotiating our world.

References

Bandura, A. (1986). *Social foundations of thought and action: A social cognitive theory*. Englewood Cliffs, NJ: Prentice-Hall.

Bandura, M., & Dweck, C. S. (1985). *The relationship of conceptions of intelligence and achievement goals to achievement-related cognition, affect and behavior*. Unpublished manuscript, Harvard University.

Bar-On, R. (2006). The Bar-On model of emotional-social intelligence (ESI). *Psiothemia, 18,* 13–25.

Beck, A. T. (1979). *Cognitive therapy of depression*. New York, NY: Guilford Press.

Beck, I. L., & McKeown, M. G. (1998). Comprehension: e sine qua non of reading. In S. Patton & M. Holmes (Eds.), *The keys to literacy* (pp. 40–52). Washington, DC: Council for Basic Education.

Beghetto, R. A. (2010). Creativity in the classroom. In J. C. Kaufman & R. J. Sternberg (Eds.), *The Cambridge handbook of creativity* (pp. 447–463). Cambridge, England: Cambridge University Press.

Brackett, M. A., Rivers, S. E., Reyes, M. R., & Salovey, P. (2012). Enhancing academic performance and social and emotional competence with the RULER feeling words curriculum. *Learning and Individual Differences, 22,* 218–224.

Chin, C. A., Anderson, R. C., & Waggoner, M. A. (2001). Patterns of discourse in two kinds of literature discussion. *Reading Research Quarterly, 30,* 378–411.

Ciarrochi, J., & Mayer, J. D. (2007). The key ingredients of emotional intelligence interventions: Similarities and differences. In J. Ciarrochi & J. D. Mayer (Eds.), *Applying emotional intelligence: A practitioner's guide* (pp. 144–156). New York, NY: Psychology Press.

Collaborative for Academic, Social, and Emotional Learning. (2013). *Effective social and emotional learning programs: Preschool and elementary school edition*. Chicago, IL: Author.

Collaborative for Academic, Social, and Emotional Learning. (2017). *Core SEL competencies*. Retrieved from https://casel.org/core-competencies

Csikszentmihalyi, M. (1991). *Flow: The psychology of optimal experience*. New York, NY: HarperCollins.

Csikszentmihalyi, M. (1996). *Creativity: Flow and the psychology of discovery and invention*. New York, NY: Harper Perennial.

Dai, D., & Speerschneider, K. (2012). Cope and grow: A model of affective curriculum for talent development. *Talent Development and Excellence, 4,* 181–199.

DeFrance, N. L., & Fahrenbruck, M. L. (2015). Constructing a plan for text-based discussion. *Journal of Adolescent & Adult Literacy, 59,* 575–585. doi:10.1002/jaal.477

Degener, S., & Berne, J. (2016). Complex questions promote complex thinking. *e Reading Teacher, 70,* 595–599. doi:10.1002/trtr.1535

Duke, N. K., Pearson, P. D., Strachan, S. L., & Billman, A. K. (2011). Essential elements of fostering and teaching reading comprehension. In S. J. Samuels & A. E. Farstrup (Eds.), *What research has to say about reading instruction* (pp. 51–93). Newark, DE: International Reading Association. doi:10.1598/0829.03

Durlak, J. A., Weissberg, R. P., Dymnicki, A. B., Taylor, R. D. & Schellinger, K. B. (2011). The impact of enhancing students' social and emotional learning: A meta-analysis of school-based universal interventions. *Child Development, 82,* 405–432.

Dweck, C. S. (2006). *Mindset: The new psychology of success.* New York, NY: Random House.

Ellis, A. R. (1997). Rational emotive behavior therapy. In C. Feltham (Ed.), *Which psychotherapy? Leading exponents explain their differences* (pp. 51–67). Thousand Oaks, CA: Sage.

Erikson, E. H. (1994). *Identity and the life cycle.* New York, NY: Norton.

Fisher, D., & Frey, N. (2012). Close reading in elementary schools. *The Reading Teacher, 66,* 179–188. doi:10.1002/TRTR.01117

Fisher, D., & Frey, N. (2014). Scaffolded reading instruction of content-area texts. *The Reading Teacher, 67,* 347–351. doi:10.1002/trtr.1234

Ford, D. Y., Tyson, C. A., Howard, T. C., & Harris III, J. J. (2000). Multicultural literature and gifted Black students: Promoting self-understanding, awareness, and pride. *Roeper Review, 22,* 235–240.

Frank, A. J., & McBee, M. T. (2003). The use of Harry Potter and the Sorcerer's Stone to discuss identity development with gifted adolescents. *Journal of Secondary Gifted Education, 15,* 33–41.

Friedman, A. A., & Cataldo, C. A. (2002). Characters at crossroads: Reflective decision makers in contemporary Newbery books: Characters in fine literature serve to model decision-making skills. *The Reading Teacher, 56,* 102–113.

Gardner, H. (2011). *Frames of mind: A theory of multiple intelligences.* New York, NY: Basic Books.

Glasser, W. (1999). *Choice theory: A new psychology of personal freedom.* New York, NY: HarperPerennial.

Goleman, D. (1995, Oct 22). Emotions: The sources of real intelligence. *The Times.* Retrieved from http://login.proxy.library.vanderbilt.edu/login?url=https://search.proquest.com/docview/318354410?accountid=14816

Gottfredson, L. S. (1996). Gottfredson's theory of circumscription and compromise. In D. Brown & L. Brooks (Eds.), *Career choice and development* (3rd ed., pp. 179–232). New York, NY: Guilford Press.

Gresham, F. M. (1995). Best practices in social skills training. In A. Thomas & J. Grimes (Eds.), *Best practices in school psychology* (Vol. III, pp. 1021–1030). Washington, DC: National Association of School Psychologists.

Halsted, J. (2009). *Some of my best friends are books: Guiding gifted readers from pre-school to high school* (3rd ed.). Scottsdale, AZ: Great Potential Press.

Hartsell, B. (2006). Teaching toward compassion: Environmental values education for secondary students. *Journal of Secondary Gifted Education, 17,* 265–271.

Harvey, S., & Goudvis, A. (2007). *Strategies that work: Teaching comprehension for understanding and engagement* (2nd ed.). Portland, ME: Stenhouse.

Hébert, T. P., & Kent, R. (1999). Nurturing social and emotional development in gifted teenagers through young adult literature. *Roeper Review, 22,* 167–171.

Hedin, L. R., & Conderman, G. (2010). Teaching students to comprehend informational text through rereading. *The Reading Teacher, 63,* 556–565. doi:10.1598/RT.63.7.3

Ingram, M. A. (2003). The use of sociocultural poetry to assist gifted students in developing empathy for the lived experiences of others. *Journal of Secondary Gifted Education, 14,* 83–92.

Lapp, D., Grant, M., Moss, B., & Johnson, K. (2013). Close reading of science texts: What's now? What's next? *The Reading Teacher, 67,* 109–119.

Lawrence, J. F., & Snow, C. E. (2011). Oral discourse and reading. In M. L. Kamil, P. D. Pearson, E. B. Moje, & P. P. Auerbach (Eds.), *Handbook of reading research* (Vol. 4, pp. 320–337). New York, NY: Routledge.

Little, C. (2017). Designing and implementing concept-based curriculum. In L. Tan, L. Ponnusamy, & C. Quek (Eds.), *Curriculum for high ability learners* (pp. 43–59). Singapore: Springer.

Marisano, D., & Shore, B. (2010). Can personal goal setting tap the potential of the gifted underachiever? *Roeper Review, 32,* 249–258.

Maslow, A. H. (1961). Peak experiences as acute identity experiences. *The American Journal of Psychoanalysis, 21,* 254–262.

Maurer, M., & Brackett, M. (2004). *Emotional literacy in the middle school. A 6-step program to promote social, emotional and academic learning.* New York, NY: Dude.

Mayer, J. D., & Salovey, P. (1995). Emotional intelligence and the construction and regulation of feelings. *Applied and preventive psychology, 4,* 197–208.

McClelland, D. C., Atkinson, J. W., Clark, R. A., & Lowell, E. L. (1953). *The achievement motive.* New York, NY: Appleton-Century-Crofts.

McCoach, B., Gable, R., & Madura, J. (2013). *Instrument development in the affective domain: School and corporate applications.* New York, NY: Springer Science + Business Media.

McInerney, D. M., & Ali, J. (2006). Multidimensional and hierarchical assessment of school motivation: Cross-cultural validation. *Educational Psychology, 26,* 717–734.

Moon, S. M. (2003). Personal talent. *High Ability Studies, 14,* 5–21.

National Governors Association. (2013). *Trends in state implementation of the Common Core State Standards: Making the shift to better tests.* Washington, DC: Author.

O'Connor, S. C., & Rosenblood, L. K. (1996). Affiliation motivation in everyday experience: A theoretical comparison. *Journal of Personality and Social Psychology, 70,* 513.

Paul, R. (1992). *Thinking skills in a changing world.* Sonoma, CA: Sonoma State University.

Peterson, D. S., & Taylor, B. M. (2012). Using higher order questioning to accelerate students' growth in reading. *The Reading Teacher, 65,* 295–304. doi:10.1002/TRTR.01045

Pink, D. (2006). *Whole new mind.* New York, NY: Penguin.

Pinker, S. (2011). *The better angels of our nature.* New York, NY: Viking.

Pressley, M., Wharton-McDonald, R., Allington, R., Block, C. C., Morrow, L., Tracey, D., . . . & Woo, D. (2001). A study of effective first-grade literacy instruction. *Scientific Studies of Reading, 5,* 35–58.

Rogers, K. (2002). *Re-forming gifted education: How parents and teachers can match the program to the child.* Scottsdale, AZ: Great Potential Press.

Rotter, J. B. (1966). Generalized expectancies for internal versus external control of reinforcement. *Psychological Monographs, 80*(1), 1–28. http://dx.doi.org/10.1037/h0092976

Santori, D., & Belfatti, M. (2017). Do text-dependent questions need to be teacher-dependent? Close reading from another angle. *The Reading Teacher, 70,* 649–657. doi:10.1002/trtr.1555

Seligman, M. E., & Csikszentmihalyi, M. (2014). Positive psychology: An introduction. In M. Csikszentmihalyi, *Flow and the foundations of positive psychology* (pp. 279–298). The Netherlands: Springer.

Seligman, M. E., Rashid, T., & Parks, A. C. (2006). Positive psychotherapy. *American Psychologist, 61,* 774.

Shaunessy, E., & Suldo, S. (2010). Strategies used by intellectually gifted students to cope with stress during their participation in a high school international baccalaureate program. *Gifted Child Quarterly, 54,* 127–137.

Stambaugh, T. (2007). *Effects of the Jacob's Ladder Reading Comprehension Program* (Unpublished doctoral dissertation). William & Mary, Williamsburg, VA.

Steenbergen-Hu, S., Makel, M. C., & Olszewski-Kubilius, P. (2016). What one hundred years of research says about the effects of ability grouping and acceleration on K–12 students' academic achievement: Findings of two second-order meta-analyses. *Review of Educational Research, 86,* 849–899. doi:10.3102/0034654316675417

Sternberg, R. J. (2006). The nature of creativity. *Creativity Research Journal, 18*(1), 87–98.

Subotnik, R. F., Olszewski-Kubilius, P., & Worrell, F. C. (2011). Rethinking giftedness and gifted education: A proposed direction forward based on psychological science. *Psychological Science in the Public Interest, 12*(1), 3–54.

Sullivan, A. K., & Strang, H. R. (2002–2003). Bibliotherapy in the class-room: Using literature to promote the development of emotional intelligence. *Childhood Education, 79,* 74–80.

Taylor, B. M., Peterson, D. S., Pearson, P. D., & Rodriguez, M. C. (2002). Looking inside classrooms: Reflecting on the "how" as well as the "what" in effective reading instruction. *The Reading Teacher, 56,* 270–279.

Vaillant, G. E. (1992). *Ego mechanisms of defense: A guide for clinicians and researchers.* Washington, DC: American Psychiatric Press.

VanTassel-Baska, J., & Little, C. (Eds.). (2017). *Content-based curriculum for gifted learners* (3rd ed.). Waco, TX: Prufrock Press.

VanTassel-Baska, J., MacIntosh, J., & Kearney, K. (2015) Secondary affective curriculum and instruction for gifted learners. In F. Dixon & S. Moon (Eds.), *Handbook of secondary gifted education* (2nd ed., pp. 513–533). Waco, TX: Prufrock Press.

VanTassel-Baska, J., & Stambaugh, T. (2006a). *Comprehensive curriculum for gifted learners* (3rd ed.). Needham Heights, MA: Allyn & Bacon.

VanTassel-Baska, J., & Stambaugh, T. (2006b). Project Athena: A pathway to advanced literacy development for children of poverty. *Gifted Child Today, 29*(2), 58–65.

Wasik, B. A., & Hindman, A. H. (2013). Realizing the promise of open-ended questions. *The Reading Teacher, 67,* 302–311. doi:10.1002/trtr.1218

Zimmerman, B. J. (2000). Self-efficacy: An essential motive to learn. *Contemporary Educational Psychology, 25*(1), 82–91.

Part II: Student Ladder Sets and Prompts

Chapter 1: Short Stories and Media
Chapter 2: Poetry
Chapter 3: Biographies, Essays, and Speeches

CHAPTER

1

Short Stories and Media

Chapter 1 includes information on the selected readings or video suggestions and accompanying question sets for each short story or media selection. Each selection is followed by two sets of questions; each set is aligned to one of the eight sets of ladder skills.

For *Affective Jacob's Ladder, Grades 4–5*, the skills covered by each selection are as follows:

Title	Ladder Skills
The Man, the Boy, and the Donkey	F, H
Wonder Trailer	G, I
Music	G, J
Eleven	E, H
The Leaping Match	G, I
Geri's Game	G, I
The Four Crafts-Men	I, K
Piper	F, G

The Man, the Boy, and the Donkey
By Aesop

A man and his son were once going with their Donkey to market. As they were walking along by its side a countryman passed them and said: "You fools, what is a Donkey for but to ride upon?"

So the Man put the Boy on the Donkey and they went on their way. But soon they passed a group of men, one of whom said: "See that lazy youngster, he lets his father walk while he rides."

So the Man ordered his Boy to get off, and got on himself. But they hadn't gone far when they passed two women, one of whom said to the other: "Shame on that lazy lout to let his poor little son trudge along."

Well, the Man didn't know what to do, but at last he took his Boy up before him on the Donkey. By this time they had come to the town, and the passers-by began to jeer and point at them. The Man stopped and asked what they were scoffing at. The men said: "Aren't you ashamed of yourself for overloading that poor Donkey of yours—you and your hulking son?"

The Man and Boy got off and tried to think what to do. They thought and they thought, till at last they cut down a pole, tied the Donkey's feet to it, and raised the pole and the Donkey to their shoulders. They went along amid the laughter of all who met them till they came to Market Bridge, when the Donkey, getting one of his feet loose, kicked out and caused the Boy to drop his end of the pole. In the struggle the Donkey fell over the bridge, and his fore-feet being tied together he was drowned.

"That will teach you," said an old man who had followed them:
The moral: "Please all and you will please none."

Facing Adversity and Challenges

F3

Rewrite the fable in a way that shows how the man and the boy could have responded in a more appropriate way to the central challenge or problem. Include a new moral that explains how to respond to the opinions of others.

Analyzing Adverse Situations and Conditions

F2

Were the challenges the man and the boy faced more internal (personal) or external (problems with other people)? What were the factors that caused the challenges?

Recognizing Adversity and Challenge

F1

What were the main challenges the man and the boy faced according to the man and the boy? According to the narrator? According to the villagers?

THE MAN, THE BOY, AND THE DONKEY

Actualizing Potential to Advance a Goal

H3

Why is it important to remember one's purpose or goal when going about a task? Write a flash fiction piece (15 words or less with a beginning, middle, and end) or a haiku (5-syllable line, 7-syllable line, 5-syllable line) about a situation you know about when the end goal was forgotten, other influences overpowered, and the situation ended poorly. (Example: It all started well, until I listened to them; now I have stitches.)

Understanding Roles and Affiliations

H2

How might the man have handled the suggestions of the villagers differently if he had different personality traits? What personality traits kept him from reaching his goal of getting the donkey to the market?

Knowing Oneself

H1

It is said that our strengths are also our weaknesses. Think about the character traits of the man. What were his strengths and weaknesses, and how does he represent this statement? Make a list of your best traits. Then, think about how they might become weaknesses and list how you might prevent that situation.

THE MAN, THE BOY, AND THE DONKEY

Wonder Trailer

Show the official movie trailer for *Wonder*, found here: https://www.youtube.com/watch?v=ZDPEKXx_lAI. Students who have read the book or seen the movie may choose to provide a brief synopsis for their classmates. Explain to students that for the purposes of the ladder questions, they do not need to watch the entire movie or read the book. They can focus on what is provided in the trailer. There is enough information from the trailer to answer the questions.

The video will need to be shown multiple times as students progress through the ladder questions. After watching the video once, provide questions for each ladder rung so that subsequent viewings can be targeted toward answering specific questions. Additional opportunities for viewing the video may be provided at a computer center if students are working independently on jotting down responses before discussing in small- or whole-group settings.

Engaging in Productive Risk-Taking

G3

What is a risk you might take to make a positive difference in your life or someone else's? For example, you could sit with someone at lunch who usually eats alone or commit to ask a question in class if you don't usually talk or raise your hand. Write down what you will do and check to see that you did it within a week.

Considering Multiple Perspectives

G2

When taking a risk, how might seeking someone else's perspective help you? How was that portrayed in the movie trailer? Whose perspectives matter to you and who might you talk to before taking a risk? Why?

Identifying and Calculating Risks

G1

Who took the bigger risk, Auggie, or the friend who sat with him at lunch? Why do you think that?

WONDER TRAILER

Collaborating With Others

I3

Work with a partner to create a poster for an ad campaign that shows ways your schoolmates can show empathy. Provide specific examples such as "Sit with someone at lunch who is alone," "Ask someone a question about their interests," "Listen to another's perspectives," "Share an idea," etc. Use ideas from the video and other sources. Now title the poster, based on what it represents.

Communicating and Responding to Others

I2

Auggie says, "If you really want to see what people are, all you have to do is look." What does he mean? What are some ways you can "look" within yourself and at others to develop empathy?

Understanding Others' Needs and Values

I1

What are some examples of empathy (identifying with the feelings of others) shown in the movie trailer? Cite examples of how different people in the trailer showed their understanding of Auggie's needs and his value as a person.

WONDER TRAILER

Music

By Arya Okten

I wriggle in my cold seat. I am bored of waiting. Then, my mother leans over and tells me to stop moving around and to be respectful. I try, I really do, but even I don't think that I succeed. Then, suddenly, as though this one thought has occupied many more moments than it should have, the woman calls my name in her high-pitched squawk. Almost immediately the pins in my feet disappear, only to be replaced by a cool sense of foreboding. I feel my mother nudge me; I have taken up too much time already. I take a gulp of air and stand up, only to have my face turn beetroot red when I see the audience staring at me. My legs take me to the front of my formidable enemy, yet friend, which is a huge black structure, made of wood, and furnished with what seems like a thousand strings. I sit on the soft leather bench, and I feel almost at home, until I feel the hundred or so pairs of eyes on my back. I take another gulp of air; it is time. My fingertips touch the edge of the smooth, hard, ivory. Beads of sweat run down my face. I am scared, but I know that in the end, I will have to face my fear. So it begins. I press the first key, then another, slowly at first, but then fast. My fingers are soon a blur, moving, and jumping like a young squirrel, but I don't care. My fingers know the routine well enough, A, G, B, and so on, but my brain is much more preoccupied. Listen, listen, that's all my brain does. Softer here, louder there, put more emotion into this part. I feel the music inside of me, pulsing, throbbing, and trying to get out. I am the pianist.

Then, all of a sudden, my song is over. My feet step lightly on the ground and after a few steps to the front of the stage my whole body bows, but in my virtual reality I am still at the piano. In my mind, I stay at the leathery seat for a few more fleeting moments, playing, but then I am back with my mother. She tells me I did great and I blush. After that the concert is a blur. I take note only of the people who played beautifully. Then, it is time to go home, but that doesn't stop me from playing. I play every day, calculating the sound of every little detail, absorbing the beautiful resonance, teaching myself how to touch the piano, so that just the right sound comes out. I will always be the pianist.

Note. Originally published in *Creative Kids* magazine, Fall 2014. Reprinted with permission by Prufrock Press.

Engaging in Productive Risk-Taking

G3

Write an original song, poem, or short piece like "Music" that tells about a time when you took a risk and how it turned out. Put it on a form of social media and comment on what it means for your audience.

music
- sub
national

Considering Multiple Perspectives

G2

How much value do you the think the pianist placed on what other people thought about the performance? What evidence in the story explains your thinking? How much value do you place on what other people think about you and your performance in a given area of endeavor? Does this ever stop you from performing? Why or why not?

Identifying and Calculating Risks

G1

What can you infer about the level of risk the pianist took to perform? Was the risk-taking necessary for the performance?

MUSIC

J3

Creating a Plan for Management

How might the stress management techniques after the performance have changed if the pianist had messed up? Rewrite the last paragraph of the story, assuming the performance did not go well, but the pianist still had a healthy response to the stressful situation.

J2

Applying Stress Control Techniques

What strategies did the pianist use to handle the stress that was felt before, during, and after the performance? What do you do? Complete the following table with examples from the text and your own experiences/example of a performance or stressful event you encountered:

Performance	Evidence From the Text	My Personal Strategies or Experiences
Before		
During		
After		

MUSIC

J1

Identifying Conditions/Situations That Cause Stress

What made this situation a potentially stressful one for the pianist? How do you feel before you have to get up in front of people to do something? Create a metaphor or an analogy that describes the feeling.

Eleven

By Sandra Cisneros

Access the YouTube video of Sandra Cisneros reading her story "Eleven" at https://www.youtube.com/watch?v=M_NaeodivR0. Before showing the video, turn on closed captioning, if available, or if you have a copy of the story for students to read and follow along with, you may distribute that.

If you don't have a copy of the story or you are focusing on speaking and listening skills, the video will need to be shown multiple times as students progress through the ladder questions. After watching the video once, provide questions for each ladder rung so that subsequent viewings can be targeted toward answering specific questions. Additional opportunities for viewing the video may be provided at a computer center if students are working independently on jotting down responses before discussing in small- or whole-group settings.

Using Emotion

E3

How could Rachel have used her emotions in a way that allowed her to have a positive voice? Create a different scenario that shows how Rachel spoke up about her sweater in a positive way. Be ready to explain how the change in Rachel's response impacts the theme of the story and Rachel's character.

Expressing Emotion

E2

What do you think Rachel's 11th birthday had to do with the way she was unable to verbally express what she was feeling? What does her 11th birthday symbolize in her mind? Describe what it means to her and create an object as a symbol for her reactions.

Understanding Emotion

E1

Why do you think Rachel isn't able to adequately express her emotions about the sweater and event? What evidence in the story suggests that?

ELEVEN

H3 Actualizing Potential to Advance a Goal

How do Rachel's beliefs about being 11 and her responses to her experiences conflict? How might Rachel identify with her younger and older self? Make a list of her reactions and explain what her younger and older self might be saying or expecting as a response.

Reactions	Older Self	Younger Self
Example: Not being able to speak up about the sweater		

Then, write one goal from the problem in the story that you think she could work on. Be specific. What steps could she take? How will she know when she is successful?

H2 Understanding Roles and Affiliations

What is the central problem in this story? Who/what does Rachel want to affiliate or associate with? Why?

H1 Knowing Oneself

Why does Rachel keep saying eleven, ten, nine, eight . . . ? What does that say about her identity?

ELEVEN

The Leaping Match

By Hans Christian Andersen

The flea, the grasshopper, and the frog once wanted to try which of them could jump highest; so they invited the whole world, and anybody else who liked, to come and see the grand sight. Three famous jumpers were they, as was seen by every one when they met together in the room.

"I will give my daughter to him who shall jump highest," said the King, "it would be too bad for you to have the trouble of jumping, and for us to offer you no prize."

The flea was the first to introduce himself; he had such polite manners, and bowed to the company on every side, for he was of noble blood; besides, he was accustomed to the society of man, which had been a great advantage to him.

Next came the grasshopper; he was not quite so slightly and elegantly formed as the flea; however, he knew perfectly well how to conduct himself, and wore a green uniform, which belonged to him by right of birth. Moreover, he declared himself to have sprung from a very ancient and honorable Egyptian family, and that in his present home he was very highly esteemed, so much so, indeed, that he had been taken out of the field and put into a card-house three stories high, built on purpose for him, and all of court-cards, the colored sides being turned inwards: as for the doors and windows in his house, they were cut out of the body of the Queen of Hearts. "And I can sing so well," added he, "that sixteen parlor-bred crickets, who have chirped and chirped ever since they were born and yet could never get anybody to build them a card-house, after hearing me have fretted themselves ten times thinner than ever, out of sheer envy and vexation!" Both the flea and the grasshopper knew excellently well how to make the most of themselves, and each considered himself quite an equal match for a princess.

The frog said not a word; however, it might be that he thought the more, and the house-dog, after going snuffing about him, confessed that the frog must be of a good family. And the old counselor, who in vain received three orders to hold his tongue, declared that the frog must be gifted with the spirit of prophecy, for that one could read on his back whether there was to be a severe or a mild winter, which, to be sure, is more than can be read on the back of the man who writes the weather almanac.

"Ah, I say nothing for the present!" remarked the old King, "but I observe everything, and form my own private opinion thereupon." And now the match began. The flea jumped so high that no one could see what had become of him, and so they insisted that he had not jumped at all, "which was disgraceful, after he had made such a fuss!"

The grasshopper only jumped half as high, but he jumped right into the King's face, and the King declared he was quite disgusted by his rudeness.

The frog stood still as if lost in thought; at last people fancied he did not intend to jump at all.

"I'm afraid he is ill!" said the dog; and he went snuffing at him again, when lo! all at once he made a little side-long jump into the lap of the Princess, who was sitting on a low stool close by.

Then spoke the King: "There is nothing higher than my daughter, therefore he who jumps up to her jumps highest; but only a person of good understanding would ever have thought of that, and thus the frog has shown us that he has understanding. He has brains in his head, that he has!"

And thus the frog won the Princess.

"I jumped highest for all that!" exclaimed the flea. "But it's all the same to me; let her have the stiff-legged, slimy creature, if she like him! I jumped highest, but I am too light and airy for this stupid world; the people can neither see me nor catch me; dullness and heaviness win the day with them!" And so the flea went into foreign service, where, it is said, he was killed.

And the grasshopper sat on a green bank, meditating on the world and its goings on, and at length he repeated the flea's last words—"Yes, dullness and heaviness win the day! dullness and heaviness win the day!" And then he again began singing his own peculiar, melancholy song, and it is from him that we have learnt this history; and yet, my friend, though you read it here in a printed book, it may not be perfectly true.

Engaging in Productive Risk-Taking

G3

What idea emerges from the tale about the concept of truth? What words/phrases are used to convey the writer's ideas about truth? Write a journal entry to express your thoughts and feelings about how telling the truth involves risk.

Considering Multiple Perspectives

G2

How does one's perception of self and others affect his or her actions? What is the risk of being self-aware? Use evidence in the story and from your own experiences to discuss this idea.

Identifying and Calculating Risks

G1

Why did the frog win the princess, according to the flea? Do you agree with that assessment? Why or why not? Assess the strengths and weaknesses of each contestant by creating a T-chart.

THE LEAPING MATCH

Collaborating With Others

I3

What does the tale provide you as a moral in how to behave? In how to relate to others? In how to accomplish what you want? Write a moral to support your ideas.

Communicating and Responding to Others

I2

What characteristics of the frog's behavior do you think allowed him to win the contest?

With which character do you identify and why?

Understanding Others' Needs and Values

I1

Which jumper (frog, flea, grasshopper) best understood the needs of others? What evidence in the story supports your idea?

THE LEAPING MATCH

Geri's Game

Written and directed by Jan Pinkava

Show students the short Pixar film entitled *Geri's Game* (available online).

The video will need to be shown more than once. After watching the video once, provide questions for each ladder rung so that subsequent viewings can be targeted toward answering specific questions. Additional opportunities for viewing the video may be provided at a computer center if students are working independently on jotting down responses before discussing in small- or whole-group settings.

Engaging in Productive Risk-Taking

G3

What skills or traits would Geri have to have in order to reach out to someone else and ask them to play chess with him? How would he approach the situation to ask someone else? What would he do if they said "no"? Create a skit of a good and bad example of how Geri might ask someone to play chess. Explain why your example is a good one.

Considering Multiple Perspectives

G2

Create a short story (with two chapters) or two monologues that portray two different perspectives of the situation—one from Geri's perspective and one from a bystander in the park who is intently staring at Geri's antics while playing chess. How do the two perspectives vary? Why do you think that is?

Identifying and Calculating Risks

G1

Why do you think Geri is playing chess by himself instead of trying to find someone to play with him?

Which is riskier—reaching out to someone and possibly being rejected or being alone and being viewed as odd or unusual?

GERI'S GAME

Collaborating With Others

l3

How might collaboration with others allow for a more productive life? When is it better to work by yourself? Use Geri's example as evidence in addition to your own ideas.

Communicating and Responding to Others

l2

Instead of playing chess by himself, what else might Geri have done to communicate his feelings and engage with others in productive ways? Brainstorm a list of at least 12 ways Geri might try to connect with others instead of playing chess by himself. Then select your best ideas and write a short letter to Geri suggesting some ways he might try to reach out to others.

Understanding Others' Needs and Values

l1

What was Geri's problem in the story? How do you know?

The Four Crafts-Men

By Jacob Grimm and Wilhelm Grimm

"Dear children," said a poor man to his four sons, "I have nothing to give you; you must go out into the wide world and try your luck. Begin by learning some craft or another, and see how you can get on." So the four brothers took their walking-sticks in their hands, and their little bundles on their shoulders, and after bidding their father good-bye, went all out at the gate together. When they had got on some way they came to four cross-ways, each leading to a different country. Then the eldest said, "Here we must part; but this day four years we will come back to this spot, and in the meantime each must try what he can do for himself."

So each brother went his way; and as the eldest was hastening on a man met him, and asked him where he was going, and what he wanted. "I am going to try my luck in the world, and should like to begin by learning some art or trade," answered he. "Then," said the man, "go with me, and I will teach you how to become the cunningest thief that ever was." "No," said the other, "that is not an honest calling, and what can one look to earn by it in the end but the gallows?" "Oh!" said the man, "you need not fear the gallows; for I will only teach you to steal what will be fair game: I meddle with nothing but what no one else can get or care anything about, and where no one can find you out." So the young man agreed to follow his trade, and he soon showed himself so clever, that nothing could escape him that he had once set his mind upon.

The second brother also met a man, who, when he found out what he was setting out upon, asked him what craft he meant to follow. "I do not know yet," said he. "Then come with me, and be a star-gazer. It is a noble art, for nothing can be hidden from you, when once you understand the stars." The plan pleased him much, and he soon became such a skillful star-gazer, that when he had served out his time, and wanted to leave his master, he gave him a glass, and said, "With this you can see all that is passing in the sky and on earth, and nothing can be hidden from you."

The third brother met a huntsman, who took him with him, and taught him so well all that belonged to hunting, that he became very clever in the craft of the woods; and when he left his master he gave him a bow, and said, "Whatever you shoot at with this bow you will be sure to hit."

The youngest brother likewise met a man who asked him what he wished to do. "Would not you like," said he, "to be a tailor?" "Oh, no!" said the young man; "sitting cross-legged from morning to night, working backwards and forwards with a needle and goose, will never suit me." "Oh!"

answered the man, "that is not my sort of tailoring; come with me, and you will learn quite another kind of craft from that." Not knowing what better to do, he came into the plan, and learnt tailoring from the beginning; and when he left his master, he gave him a needle, and said, "you can sew anything with this, be it as soft as an egg or as hard as steel; and the joint will be so fine that no seam will be seen."

After the space of four years, at the time agreed upon, the four brothers met at the four cross-roads; and having welcomed each other, set off towards their father's home, where they told him all that had happened to them, and how each had learned some craft.

Then, one day, as they were sitting before the house under a very high tree, the father said, "I should like to try what each of you can do in this way." So he looked up, and said to the second son, "At the top of this tree there is a chaffinch's nest; tell me how many eggs there are in it." The stargazer took his glass, looked up, and said, "Five." "Now," said the father to the eldest son, "take away the eggs without letting the bird that is sitting upon them and hatching them know anything of what you are doing." So the cunning thief climbed up the tree, and brought away to his father the five eggs from under the bird; and it never saw or felt what he was doing, but kept sitting on at its ease. Then the father took the eggs, and put one on each corner of the table, and the fifth in the middle; and said to the huntsman, "Cut all the eggs in two pieces at one shot." The huntsman took up his bow, and at one shot struck all the five eggs as his father wished. "Now comes your turn," said he to the young tailor; "sew the eggs and the young birds in them together again, so neatly that the shot shall have done them no harm." Then the tailor took his needle, and sewed the eggs as he was told; and when he had done, the thief was sent to take them back to the nest, and put them under the bird without its knowing it. Then she went on sitting, and hatched them: and in a few days they crawled out, and had only a little red streak across their necks, where the tailor had sewn them together.

"Well done, sons!" said the old man: "you have made good use of your time, and learnt something worth the knowing; but I am sure I do not know which ought to have the prize. Oh! that a time might soon come for you to turn your skill to some account!"

Not long after this there was a great bustle in the country; for the king's daughter had been carried off by a mighty dragon, and the king mourned over his loss day and night, and made it known that whoever brought her back to him should have her for a wife. Then the four brothers said to each other, "Here is a chance for us; let us try what we can do." And they agreed to see whether they could not set the princess free. "I will soon find out where she is, however," said the star-gazer, as he looked through his glass: and he soon cried out, "I see her afar off, sitting upon a rock in the sea; and I can spy the dragon close by, guarding her." Then he went to the king, and asked for a ship for himself and his brothers; and they sailed together over the sea, till they came to the right place. There they found the princess sitting, as the star-gazer had said, on the rock; and the dragon was lying asleep, with his head upon her lap. "I dare not shoot at him," said the huntsman, "for I should kill the beautiful young lady also." "Then I will try my skill," said the thief; and went and stole her away from under the dragon, so quietly and gently that the beast did not know it, but went on snoring.

Then away they hastened with her full of joy in their boat towards the ship; but soon came the dragon roaring behind them through the air; for he awoke and missed the princess. But when he got over the boat, and wanted to pounce upon them and carry off the princess, the huntsman took up his bow and shot him straight through the heart, so that he fell down dead. They were still not safe; for he was such a great beast that in his fall he overset the boat, and they had to swim in the open sea upon a few planks. So the tailor took his needle, and with a few large stitches put some of the planks together; and he sat down upon these, and sailed about and gathered up all the pieces of the boat; and then tacked them together so quickly that the boat was soon ready, and they then reached the ship and got home safe.

When they had brought home the princess to her father, there was great rejoicing; and he said to the four brothers, "One of you shall marry her, but you must settle amongst yourselves which it is to be." Then there arose a quarrel between them; and the star-gazer said, "If I had not found the princess out, all your skill would have been of no use; therefore she ought to be my wife." "Your seeing her would have been of no use," said the thief, "if I had not taken her away from the dragon; therefore she ought to be my wife." "No, she is my beloved," said the huntsman; "for if I had not killed the dragon, he would, after all, have torn you and the princess into pieces." "And if I had not sewn the boat together again," said the tailor, "you would all have been drowned; therefore she is to be my wife." Then the king put in a word, and said, "Each of you is right; and as all cannot marry the young lady, the best way is for neither of you to have her hand in marriage: for the truth is, there is somebody she likes a great deal better. But to make up for your loss, I will give each of you, as a reward for his skill, half a kingdom." So the brothers agreed that this plan would be much better than either quarrelling or marrying a lady who had no mind to have them. And the king then gave to each half a kingdom, as he had said; and they lived very happily the rest of their days, and took good care of their father; and somebody took better care of the young lady, than to let either the dragon or one of the Crafts-men marry her.

Collaborating With Others

I3

Create a moral for the story about the relationship between collaboration and success, using the craftsmen's collective feats as evidence. Apply your moral to your own life. How have you collaborated with others to bring about a greater good?

Communicating and Responding to Others

I2

The princess is rescued because the craftsmen express empathy for her situation. How do they demonstrate their feelings? Does the ending of the story show empathy or greed? What makes you think that?

What examples of empathy have you illustrated in your life?

Understanding Others' Needs and Values

I1

What were the needs of the craftsmen in the story? What about the princess? The father? The king?

THE FOUR CRAFTS-MEN

Reflecting on Patterns of Achievement

K3

What accomplishments have meant the most to you so far in life? What processes and strategies did you use to reach your goal? Create a blueprint of your road to success by writing down the plan that has worked for you.

Assessing Strengths and Interests

K2

How did the brothers meet their goal of becoming proficient in a craft? What skills did they practice?

Identifying Barriers to Achievement

K1

What barriers did the brothers encounter as they tried to become proficient at a craft? What strategies did they use to overcome them?

THE FOUR CRAFTS-MEN

Piper

Written and directed by Alan Barillaro

Show students the short Pixar film entitled *Piper* (available online).

The video will need to be shown more than once. After watching the video once, provide questions for each ladder rung so that subsequent viewings can be targeted toward answering specific questions. Additional opportunities for viewing the video may be provided at a computer center if students are working independently on jotting down responses before discussing in small- or whole-group settings.

F3

Facing Adversity and Challenges

Create a character that provides a monologue on how to handle adversity based on what you learned from the video. Which ideas are most important to stress and why?

F2

Analyzing Adverse Situations and Conditions

What strategies and personal characteristics did the bird employ to overcome the challenges it faced? How might you apply these same strategies and personal characteristics to help you overcome an adverse situation or challenge in your life? Complete a 3-column chart.

Bird's Personal Characteristics	Strategies the Bird Employs	Situations in Your Life

PIPER

F1

Recognizing Adversity and Challenge

Create a list of the figurative and literal problems the bird faced. Look through your list and compare it with a classmate's list. Together, discuss the following question: What was the main problem the bird had to face? Explain your thinking, using evidence from the video.

Figurative Problems	Literal Problems

Engaging in Productive Risk-Taking

G3

How might one's emotions be a help or hindrance when taking a risk? Write a lesson or set of rules that might help someone else decide when he or she should give in to fears because it is an unsafe choice versus when he or she should push through fears and overcome obstacles. Use examples from your life, conversations with your family, other books you have read, and the video to help you write your response.

Considering Multiple Perspectives

G2

How did the bird's observance of other perspectives help it manage the risks it faced? Look at your plot map from G1. What do you notice about the emotions the bird might have been feeling before and after considering multiple perspectives?

PIPER

Identifying and Calculating Risks

G1

Create a plot map of important events and actions of the young bird's life. Label the emotions you think the bird was feeling as a result of each action (or risk) in the video.

CHAPTER

2

Poetry

Chapter 2 includes selected poems and accompanying question sets for each selection. Each selection is followed by one or two sets of ladders and subsequent questions; each set is aligned to one of the eight sets of affective ladder skills.

For *Affective Jacob's Ladder, Grades 4–5*, the skills covered by each selection are as follows:

Title	Ladder Skills
Success Is Counted Sweeter	K, L
Mending	K, L
The Fool's Song	E, J
Casey at the Bat	J, L
A Lazy Day	E, J
Winter Branches	E
From a Bridge Car	E

Success Is Counted Sweetest

By Emily Dickinson

Success is counted sweetest
By those who ne'er succeed.
To comprehend a Nectar
Requires sorest need.
Not one of all the Purple Host
Who took the Flag to-day,
Can tell the definition
So plain, of Victory
As he defeated, dying,
On whose forbidden ear
The distant strains of triumph
Break, agonizing clear.

Reflecting on Patterns of Achievement

K3

The character (one of the "purple Host") in Dickinson's poem dies in the final stanza even as he defeats the enemy. What qualities has he exhibited? Would you ascribe success to his action? Why or why not?

Assessing Strengths and Interests

K2

What assets might we infer were employed to defeat the enemy? Is the use of force ever not justified if it brings a desirable outcome? Debate with your partner.

Identifying Barriers to Achievement

K1

What barriers do soldiers face in battle? Make a list of at least 10, half under the heading "physical" and the other half under the heading "mental" and then list the top three. Discuss with your partner why you have more in one column than the other.

SUCCESS IS COUNTED SWEETEST

L3

Demonstrating High-Level Performance in a Given Area

Some people have stated that to be successful, one must have a deep personal need that requires fulfilling. How does the first stanza of the poem view success? What is your view on this issue? Take a stand that defines the criteria you apply to being successful and defend it, using your understanding of the poem and circumstances you have encountered in life.

Applying Learning to Practice

L2

What are the steps to take in becoming successful in a battle, do you think? In life? What is Dickinson's view of the process? How does one become a hero in our culture?

Recognizing Internal and External Factors That Promote Talent Development

L1

What is success? How is it attained? These are questions of interest to everybody at different stages of development. Describe what success looks like to you in a brief statement. What object or symbol would you say most signifies success for you? Why?

SUCCESS IS COUNTED SWEETEST

Mending

By Hazel Hall

Here are old things:
Fraying edges,
Ravelling threads;
And here are scraps of new goods,
Needles and thread,
An expectant thimble,
A pair of silver-toothed scissors.
Thimble on a finger,
New thread through an eye;
Needle, do not linger,
Hurry as you ply.
If you ever would be through
Hurry, scurry, fly!
Here are patches,
Felled edges,
Darned threads,
Strengthening old utility,
Pending the coming of the new.
Yes, I have been mending . . .
But also,
I have been enacting
A little travesty on life.

Discuss the following aspects of the poem with a partner before beginning the ladders provided:

- What is "a travesty" that the poet mentions in the last line of the poem? What does she mean?

- What are the words in the poem that relate to the act of sewing? Make a list of them.

- How does the act of sewing accommodate new and old things?

- Why does the sewing take on the feeling of urgency? What in life is urgent?

- How is mending (or sewing) in the poem a metaphor for life? What examples support your ideas?

K3

Reflecting on Patterns of Achievement

Many people allow life to just happen to them serendipitously. Others plan for specific occurrences. How do you think about your future? Assuming you want to plan for your formal education as a prelude to a career, what are the markers that you would want to experience? Develop an educational plan that begins where you are now and takes you into a professional career. Use the template provided below to "sew in" the relevant pieces and reflect on the pattern you create:

Level	Key Events	Skills I Want to Develop	Accomplishments
Elementary School			
Middle School			
High School			
College			
Career			

Assessing Strengths and Interests

K2

What do you perceive to be your major strengths and areas for improvement? Make a list and describe how your strengths might be used to improve your weaknesses.

Identifying Barriers to Achievement

K1

What barriers would keep you from sewing the life that you might like? Name three and think about how they might be overcome.

MENDING

Demonstrating High-Level Performance in a Given Area

L3

In what ways does the poet relate the idea of creating a life to the act of sewing? In a chart, show what the relationship might be.

Creating a Life	Act of Sewing

Then, create a collage that "sews together" the pieces of your life to date. What might your collage look like in 10 years? Compare and contrast each version.

Applying Learning to Practice

L2

How can the factors from L1 work together to help you achieve your dreams? For example, how can the quality of persistence be applied to your education? Write an essay that integrates at least three of the factors and describes how they fit together.

Recognizing Internal and External Factors That Promote Talent Development

L1

What are the factors that you would "sew into your life" that might aid you in developing your abilities and aptitudes to optimal levels? Select from the following list and note how they might aid you.

Factors	How They Are Useful?
Parents	
Motivation levels	
Friends	
Persistence	
Positive outlook (optimism)	
Determination	
Education	
Life experiences (e.g., travel, living in different places)	

MENDING

The Fool's Song

By William Carlos Williams

I tried to put a bird in a cage.
O fool that I am!
For the bird was Truth.
Sing merrily, Truth: I tried to put
Truth in a cage!
    And when I had the bird in the cage,
O fool that I am!
Why, it broke my pretty cage.
Sing merrily, Truth: I tried to put
Truth in a cage!
    And when the bird was flown from the cage,
O fool that I am!
Why, I had nor bird nor cage.
Sing merrily, Truth: I tried to put
Truth in a cage!
Heigh-ho! Truth in a cage.

Using Emotion

E3

Why is the phrase *caged truth* an oxymoron (i.e., a two-word contradiction in terms, such as *clearly confused, act naturally, open secret*)? What other oxymorons come to mind that could be applied to create an emotion in the poem? Create one and describe why it might be effective.

Expressing Emotion

E2

Rewrite the poem to reflect another feeling, caused by the same series of events. What emotion have you portrayed, and how has it changed the poem?

Understanding Emotion

E1

The poet expresses emotions about his act. What emotions does he feel about himself and why?

THE FOOL'S SONG

J3

Creating a Plan for Management

How might the poet have better managed the concept of truth than by making it a bird and putting it in a cage? What would you have done? Create your own image of truth and how you would represent it.

J2

Applying Stress Control Techniques

How might the stress portrayed in the poem have been avoided? What measures can you take to avoid stressful situations or reduce them?

J1

Identifying Conditions/Situations That Cause Stress

What stress is the narrator of the poem feeling?
What evidence supports your answer?

What factors cause stress in your life? What kinds
of situations do you experience as stressful?

THE FOOL'S SONG

Casey at the Bat
By Ernest Lawrence Thayer

The outlook wasn't brilliant for the Mudville nine that day;
the score stood four to two, with but one inning more to play.
And then when Cooney died at first, and Barrows did the same,
a sickly silence fell upon the patrons of the game.

A straggling few got up to go in deep despair. The rest
clung to that hope which springs eternal in the human breast;
they thought, if only Casey could get but a whack at that—
they'd put up even money, now, with Casey at the bat.

But Flynn preceded Casey, as did also Jimmy Blake,
and the former was a lulu and the latter was a cake,
so upon that stricken multitude grim melancholy sat,
for there seemed but little chance of Casey's getting to the bat.

But Flynn let drive a single, to the wonderment of all,
and Blake, the much despised, tore the cover off the ball;
and when the dust had lifted, and the men saw what had occurred,
there was Jimmy safe at second and Flynn a-hugging third.

Then from five thousand throats and more there rose a lusty yell;
it rumbled through the valley, it rattled in the dell;
it knocked upon the mountain and recoiled upon the flat,
for Casey, mighty Casey, was advancing to the bat.

There was ease in Casey's manner as he stepped into his place;
there was pride in Casey's bearing and a smile on Casey's face.
And when, responding to the cheers, he lightly doffed his hat,
no stranger in the crowd could doubt 'twas Casey at the bat.

Ten thousand eyes were on him as he rubbed his hands with dirt;
five thousand tongues applauded when he wiped them on his shirt.
Then while the writhing pitcher ground the ball into his hip,
defiance gleamed in Casey's eye, a sneer curled Casey's lip.

And now the leather-covered sphere came hurtling through the air,
and Casey stood a-watching it in haughty grandeur there.
Close by the sturdy batsman the ball unheeded sped—
"That ain't my style," said Casey. "Strike one," the umpire said.

From the benches, black with people, there went up a muffled roar,
like the beating of the storm-waves on a stern and distant shore.
"Kill him! Kill the umpire!" shouted someone on the stand;
and it's likely they'd have killed him had not Casey raised his hand.

With a smile of Christian charity great Casey's visage shone;
he stilled the rising tumult; he bade the game go on;
he signaled to the pitcher, and once more the spheroid flew;
but Casey still ignored it, and the umpire said: "Strike two."

"Fraud!" cried the maddened thousands, and echo answered fraud;
but one scornful look from Casey and the audience was awed.
They saw his face grow stern and cold, they saw his muscles strain,
and they knew that Casey wouldn't let that ball go by again.

The sneer is gone from Casey's lip, his teeth are clenched in hate;
he pounds with cruel violence his bat upon the plate.
And now the pitcher holds the ball, and now he lets it go,
and now the air is shattered by the force of Casey's blow.

Oh, somewhere in this favored land the sun is shining bright;
the band is playing somewhere, and somewhere hearts are light,
and somewhere men are laughing, and somewhere children shout;
but there is no joy in Mudville—mighty Casey has struck out.

J3

Creating a Plan for Management

What should Casey do next? How should he handle his strikeout? Tell a classmate your thoughts. Then complete the chart below by reframing negative reactions into something positive and productive. An example has been provided for you.

Negative Reaction	Productive Reframe
I have let everyone down.	I have a great hitting record, but missed that one. I will keep practicing.
You knew better than to swing at that pitch.	
You are no longer a good ball player.	

J2

Applying Stress Control Techniques

Reread the four lines of the poem beginning with "There was ease in Casey's manner as he stepped into his place." Was Casey overconfident? Why or why not?

How might Casey's self-confidence help him manage the stress of his situation both before going to bat and after he struck out? Write a true statement about how self-confidence can play a role in stress management. Consider using some of the following words in your statement: success, confidence, belief, stress, failure, anxiety, or perfectionism.

J1

Identifying Conditions/Situations That Cause Stress

What about Casey's situation might cause you stress? If you were in this situation, would your stress be more about trying to live up to other people's expectations or not meeting your own personal goals? Compare your ideas with that of a classmate.

CASEY AT THE BAT

Demonstrating High-Level Performance in a Given Area

L3

Is Casey a great player? What evidence in the poem supports your answer? What criteria would/did you use to judge? Conduct a quick debate with your class.

Applying Learning to Practice

L2

What lesson can be learned from this poem about elite players and their performance? About self-confidence?

CASEY AT THE BAT

Recognizing Internal and External Factors That Promote Talent Development

L1

What factors contributed to Casey's success as a batter? How might one's strength also be his or her weakness? Use evidence from the poem to support your answer.

A Lazy Day

By Paul Laurence Dunbar

The trees bend down along the stream,
Where anchored swings my tiny boat.
The day is one to drowse and dream
And list the thrush's throttling note.
When music from his bosom bleeds
Among the river's rustling reeds.

No ripple stirs the placid pool,
When my adventurous line is cast,
A truce to sport, while clear and cool,
The mirrored clouds slide softly past.
The sky gives back a blue divine,
And all the world's wide wealth is mine.

A pickerel leaps, a bow of light,
The minnows shine from side to side.
The first faint breeze comes up the tide—
I pause with half uplifted oar,
While night drifts down to claim the shore.

Using Emotion

E3

Rewrite the poem, using your own images and feelings as the basis. What will you title it? Why?

Expressing Emotion

E2

Think about a time when you have had similar feelings as those portrayed in the poem. Describe that time, event, and other aspects of the situation that helped develop your feelings. Make your description as powerful in the use of emotional language as Dunbar has done.

Understanding Emotion

E1

Write down descriptive words (individual and phrases) that Dunbar uses to depict the scene. What feelings emerge as you enter the poet's world? In a second column, make a list of words that describe your feelings about the poem.

Poet's Words	Feelings Conveyed

Creating a Plan for Management

J3

Create a model plan for stress reduction, based partly on your reading of the poem and ideas you get from it, but also from other sources. What stress reducers would you include in your plan? Be sure to read three other sources about how to manage stress.

Applying Stress Control Techniques

J2

What additional choices in activities might you make to further reduce stress?

Identifying Conditions/Situations That Cause Stress

J1

The poet has presented a scene that is often seen to reduce and remove stress. What aspects of the poem appear to be an antidote to stress? Make a list and share with your partner.

Winter Branches

By Margaret Widdemer

When winter-time grows weary, I lift my eyes on high
And see the black trees standing, stripped clear against the sky;

They stand there very silent, with the cold flushed sky behind,
The little twigs flare beautiful and restful and kind;

Clear-cut and certain they rise, with summer past,
For all that trees can ever learn they know now, at last;

Slim and black and wonderful, with all unrest gone by,
The stripped tree-boughs comfort me, drawn clear against the sky.

Using Emotion

E3

There are many poems and paintings about nature, including this one. Why might this be? What is it about nature that evokes emotion, do you think? Create a statement about nature that reflects your views on its relationship to emotion.

Expressing Emotion

E2

Apply the poet's feelings to another scene in nature that you create and describe. Write a poem or an essay, paint a picture, or compose or select a piece of music that conveys that feeling, using deliberate techniques to convey emotion. Be prepared to share your piece and explain the techniques you used and what these symbolized (i.e., contrasting colors, shading, personification, tempo, rhythm, metaphors, etc.)

Understanding Emotion

E1

Why is the narrator comforted by the sight of the "stripped tree boughs"?

What feelings do they produce in her? What aspects of the trees produce positive feelings? Identify those words or phrases.

WINTER BRANCHES

From a Bridge Car

By Elias Lieberman

River inscrutable, river mysterious,
    Mornings or evenings, in gray skies or blue,
Thousands of toilers in gay mood or serious,
    Workward and homeward have gazed upon you.

Swirling or sluggish, but ever inscrutable,
    Sparkling or oily, but never the same;
You, like the city, mysterious, mutable,
    Tremble with passions which no one can name.

Using Emotion

E3

The river is personified by the poet in this poem, meaning it is given human characteristics and behaves as a human being. Provide evidence from the poem to support that claim.

Create a poem about an aspect of nature and use personification as Lieberman has in this poem to describe it. Now draw the image of nature you have created and give both the poem and the picture a title. What have you selected and why?

Expressing Emotion

E2

Identify words or phrases used by the poet to express the narrator's emotion about the river. What are the feelings? What does the river symbolize?

Understanding Emotion

E1

Identify the most powerful words used to describe the river. What characterization do they provide? How do they make you feel?

FROM A BRIDGE CAR

CHAPTER
3

Biographies, Essays, and Speeches

Chapter 3 includes videos or selected readings and accompanying question sets for each biographical or nonfiction selection. Each selection is followed by two sets of questions; each set is aligned to one of the eight sets of affective ladder skills.

For *Affective Jacob's Ladder, Grades 4–5*, the skills covered by each selection are as follows:

Title	Ladder Skills
Engineers: Failure and Success	G, L
The Buddy Bench	E, F
A Literary Lesson on Making Mistakes	G, J
Girls in STEM	G, K
Otis Boykin	F, K
Stress Is Not the Enemy	J, K
Jacqueline Woodson	F, K
Lou Gehrig Farewell Speech	F, H
A Happy Life	F, K

Engineers: Failure and Success

Show the following two videos before asking students to respond to the subsequent ladders. As they watch the videos, tell them to think about how the lessons in engineering can apply to their own life goals, successes, and failures.

- *Succeed by Failing, Crash Course Kids*—https://www.youtube.com/watch?v=TcUX6eNT2j4

- *Defining Success, Crash Course Kids*—https://www.youtube.com/watch?v=XyFUqFQfl30

After watching the videos once, provide specific questions for each ladder rung so that subsequent viewings can be targeted toward answering specific questions. Additional opportunities for viewing the video may be provided at a computer center if students are working independently on jotting down responses before discussing in small- or whole-group settings.

Engaging in Productive Risk-Taking

G3

Does one have to take risks in order to achieve something great? Write a three-paragraph opinion piece that includes examples from what you have learned about engineers and their work, books you have read, and your own life experiences to answer this question.

Considering Multiple Perspectives

G2

Why might multiple perspectives be helpful when designing solutions or solving problems, based on the way engineers do their work? When might you consider multiple perspectives before taking a risk or designing/doing something important?

Identifying and Calculating Risks

G1

How do engineers recognize strengths and weaknesses in their plans, according to the videos?

ENGINEERS: FAILURE AND SUCCESS

Demonstrating High-Level Performance in a Given Area

L3

Why does selection of criteria matter to engineers? Why aren't their criteria the same for every problem and solution? What criteria do you use to measure your successes and failure points? Create a list of criteria you will use to determine success for a specific goal you are trying to achieve. Analyze why each criterion is important.

Applying Learning to Practice

L2

What lessons about engineering failure points and definitions of success can we apply to our own failures and successes? Write a statement about what we can learn from engineers in the form of a moral.

Recognizing Internal and External Factors That Promote Talent Development

L1

Why do engineers need to know the limitations of a structure or design? Why is it helpful to know your own limitations? Describe a situation where you encountered your own limitations and how you handled it.

ENGINEERS: FAILURE AND SUCCESS

The Buddy Bench

Show students the video listed below about the Buddy Bench or find information about Buddy Benches to help students answer the questions provided.

- How Little People Can Make a Big Difference, Charlie Cooper, TEDx JCUCairns—https://www.youtube.com/watch?v=V7Z-Hq-xvxM

Note. It may be helpful to conduct a quick search on Buddy Benches if teachers or students are not familiar with the concept so that more background knowledge can be provided. A simple browser search using the words "buddy bench" will provide a plethora of information.

After asking the students to watch the video once (or a different one of your choosing), provide students with the questions for each ladder rung so that subsequent viewings can be targeted to answering specific questions. Additional opportunities for viewing the video may be provided at a computer center if students are working independently or jotting down responses before discussing in small- or whole-group settings.

Using Emotion

E3

Think about a time when you were very angry and converted your feelings into something positive. Create your own 2-minute speech that explains how your emotions were channeled into a positive change for yourself or someone else.

Expressing Emotion

E2

How did Charlie express his emotions in healthy ways? Identify at least four ways. Make a list of some positive ways you can express your emotions about a particular event or situation.

Understanding Emotion

E1

Why is it important to understand your emotions? How did Charlie's ability to recognize and name his emotions help him come up with a positive solution?

THE BUDDY BENCH

Facing Adversity and Challenges

F3

Charlie was able to take some of the negative experiences he faced and turn them into a positive solution by instituting the Buddy Bench in his school. Think about some problems you face. Make a list. Which problems are within your control and which ones are controlled by your response? Categorize your problems accordingly. Then, create a plan of action for managing your problems or challenges in a positive way, using the following chart:

Problem	Alternative Solution Ideas	Steps Toward the Solution	Timeline

Analyzing Adverse Situations and Conditions

F2

What strategies did Charlie use to help him determine the main problem or negative conditions that were hindering his success? Think about problems you face and how you think about them. How do you decide what a main problem is when you are faced with multiple ones? Describe your strategy to a classmate.

Recognizing Adversity and Challenge

F1

What challenges did Charlie face? Make a list of all of the problems he encountered. Which ones could he manage or change? Which ones were out of his control?

A Literary Lesson on Making Mistakes

By Madeleine Deisen

Anne of Green Gables has been one of my favorite books ever since I first picked it up. Every book in that series holds a special place in my heart; they are books I can return to again and again and enjoy to the fullest each time. But Anne Shirley's adventures haven't only brought me countless hours of joy, they have also taught me a valuable lesson: It is okay to make mistakes.

For a perfectionist like myself, this lesson meant the world. I would never in a million years have tried anything without having watched somebody else do it first, because I was afraid I wouldn't do it right. Craft projects were a disaster. I expected everything I made to turn out exactly like it did on the box, even if it wasn't humanly possible with the materials and whatever I made was pretty, too. When I didn't win a ribbon at the craft fair, I felt like I would never be able to do something worthwhile. I was always hesitant to guess on tests, afraid I would be wrong, when in reality I could easily have ended up right. My perfectionism made fun things upsetting and prevented me from possible success.

Anne helped me tremendously to step away from this perfectionism. She is never afraid to try something new. She dives right in to any new task or activity set before her, no matter how daunting. Her will to learn and her never-ending curiosity fuel her constant trial and error. If she messes up, she picks herself up and goes on with it, and always does better the next time. When Anne baked a cake with medicine instead of vanilla, or jumped on the spare room bed that her friend's Aunt Josephine was lying in, or almost drowned pretending to be the Lady of Shalott, she proved that making mistakes is just a way to learn from them. As she said to Marilla, at least once she made a mistake she would never make it again.

Anne showed me that making mistakes is not so bad after all. Making a mistake only means that you tried and that you learned. If it wasn't for Anne Shirley, I would probably still be an unhealthy perfectionist, and I certainly would miss out on a lifelong friend.

Note. Originally published in *Creative Kids* magazine, Winter 2016–2017. Reprinted with permission by Prufrock Press.

Engaging in Productive Risk-Taking

G3

Create a situation where you might take an intellectual risk that you normally wouldn't, such as raising your hand to answer a question in class, providing an opinion on something that you believe in, or trying a math problem or book that is more challenging than normal. Describe how you feel about taking the risk, describing the potential positive and negative aspects of doing so.

Intellectual Risk	Advantages	Disadvantages

Considering Multiple Perspectives

G2

Is learning worth the mistakes involved? Why or why not? Write a journal entry to answer this question from the perspective of the author and an opposing view. Conclude the journal entry with your own opinion.

Identifying and Calculating Risks

G1

When is risk-taking healthy? Why? Make a list of the top three mistakes you have made in your life that resulted from taking a risk or not taking one, and what you have learned from each.

Creating a Plan for Management

J3

Create an ad or meme that advocates for reading as a way to learn about yourself and help you make good choices. Be sure to capture the theme of this reading in your ad.

Applying Stress Control Techniques

J2

How can reading books and identifying with characters help us manage stress or perfectionism? Think about a favorite book character you identify with. What makes that character so identifiable? What lessons did you learn from the character that could be applied to your life? Write your own three-paragraph essay, similar to this reading, to explain how you have identified with a character and the impact it had you.

Identifying Conditions/Situations That Cause Stress

J1

Why do you think the author was so perfectionistic? How are you similar to or different from her and how she approached projects before reading the book? Create a Venn diagram to illustrate the comparison.

A LITERARY LESSON ON MAKING MISTAKES

Girls in STEM
By Karishma Muthukumar

In this day and age, stereotypes still have a huge impact on decisions and thoughts of an individual. This can sometimes affect an entire group—comparable to a drop of ink in a crystal clear glass of water. Stereotypes are indeed powerful, and can be negative. And when a girl doubts (even just for a moment) whether she is capable of pursuing her interests and dreams, this becomes entirely a different situation.

The perceived image of a girl is almost as a storybook princess or a doll: dainty, fearful, and overly conscious. However, girls don't need to be this way; girls have unimaginable potential and should believe in themselves to achieve their dreams. This same concept applies to girls when choosing a career that is, in reality, a life decision. Unfortunately, this "doll-like" mindset may sway a girl from choosing a career in science, technology, engineering, and math (STEM), as she may be doubtful of her capabilities.

Instead of being influenced by images or ideas that are deeply rooted inside one's brain, girls must understand that STEM is not only for a certain gender. Girls should learn to "see" themselves in a STEM field. Stereotypes about girls have made it difficult for girls to visualize themselves working as a scientist, a mathematician, or even an engineer. Media, like newspapers and TV shows, in addition to verbal communication, convolute a girl's mind into thinking that it is impossible—far from reality—for her to pursue a career in STEM, which eventually distances her from even considering the option. It is apparent that the effects of this stereotyping actually exist: My mom was one of two girls in her entire computer science class in college.

Girls should pursue their aspirations rather than feeling restricted or avoiding a certain direction. A lot of women were successful and *proved* to the entire world that women can indeed be leaders in the STEM field.

- Sally Ride was the first American woman in space.
- The cofounder of Flickr is a woman named Caterina Fake.
- Maria Klawe was the fifth Harvey Mudd College President.
- The U.S. Surgeon General of 1990–1993 was Antonia Coello Novello.
- Esther Takeuchi was the recipient of the National Medal of Technology and Innovation.
- The current Facebook Chief Operating Officer is Sheryl Sandberg.
- Marissa Mayer is the president and CEO of Yahoo.
- Jane Goodall is well known for her work with chimpanzees.

- Marie Curie experimented with radioactivity and discovered the element radium.
- Rosalind Franklin's X-ray crystallography was crucial to the discovery of DNA's structure.

Girls should open up to a vast variety of choices and keep in mind that it is possible to reach any level of success with dedication and determination. Moreover, everyone should be able to contribute his or her knowledge to the world. With this added knowledge, think about the novel innovations that will be made possible; just imagine the future.

Note. Originally published in *Creative Kids* magazine, Summer 2015, Reprinted with permission by Prufrock Press.

Engaging in Productive Risk-Taking

G3

Several accomplishments of women in STEM fields are listed in the article. Select one and research its impact on humanity. Write an essay that answers the following questions: What benefits has it caused? What positive outcomes have accrued to the society? What new pathway has it forged for future researchers?

Considering Multiple Perspectives

G2

What risks have you taken to learn more than was required? What multiple perspectives have you consulted to gain more insight? For example, have you read more books on a topic, asked experts about the topic, or worked with the topic in a particular way? Specify what perspectives you considered and how they helped you.

Identifying and Calculating Risks

G1

What is intellectual risk-taking? How does it make you feel when you do it? Connect your feelings to the text.

GIRLS IN STEM

K3

Reflecting on Patterns of Achievement

In most STEM fields, there are fewer females than males. Why might this be, according to the article? Your own observations?

Research what characteristics are needed for STEM careers and link them to your personal assessment of strengths and weaknesses. Prepare a letter asking for a job in STEM and highlighting your attributes. What observations do you have about the match between your strengths and the requirements of a career in a STEM field?

Assessing Strengths and Interests

K2

Make a list of what you like to do, another one that indicates what you are good at doing, and a third that lists what you think is important to do. How do these lists relate to each other? Write a paragraph describing their points of convergence.

Identifying Barriers to Achievement

K1

Explore possible careers in STEM that interest you. Make three columns for each career, indicating characteristics required to be successful, how these characteristics relate to you, and barriers you will face.

Career	Characteristics to Be Successful	Relationship to You	Barriers You Will Face

GIRLS IN STEM

Otis Boykin

Otis Boykin was a Black inventor who improved resistor models, allowing for faster development of 20th-century electronics. Our electronic devices today still use variations of his electrical resistors. He also worked on the pacemaker, a device that has saved thousands of lives. Although he encountered difficulties in his schooling and his career, he persevered and developed more than 24 patents.

Boykin was born in 1920 in Dallas, TX. He came from a modest household with a small income. His father worked as a carpenter and eventually became a minister. Boykin's mother was a maid, but because she died quite early in his life, he never knew her. Although little is known about his childhood, it is clear that Boykin was an intelligent child with an inquisitive mind. He attended a segregated high school and earned high grades. When he graduated as valedictorian, he earned a scholarship to attend Fisk University, a highly esteemed, historically Black college in Nashville, TN.

At college, Boykin continued to excel in his engineering studies. He also worked as a lab assistant at Fisk's aeronautics lab, testing automated aircraft controls. After he graduated in 1941, he moved to Chicago, IL, to work at the Majestic Radio and TV Corporation. Because of his skill and hard work at the corporation, he was promoted to a supervisory position. A few years later, Boykin began working at P.J. Nilsen Research Labs. Soon after, he started his own research and consulting firm, Boykin-Fruth, Inc.

In 1946, Boykin pursued graduate studies at the Illinois Institute of Technology, but he was unable to continue after just one year. He could not afford the tuition, and his family was unable to support him financially. Leaving school was a great disappointment for Boykin. He wanted to be able to learn more about technology to help him with his inventions. However, he soon decided that a lack of a master's degree would not prevent him from inventing. The field of technology was blooming at the time, and he knew that with hard work and determination, he could take part in the revolution.

As he did consulting work in Chicago, he began to invent on his own time in the growing field of electronics. He soon invented several successful variations on resistors. A resistor is a part of a device that slows or impedes the flow of the electrical current in a circuit. This is important to ensure that a device receives the correct and safe amount of current. Different devices require different amounts of resistance depending on what tasks they perform. Boykin wanted to improve upon the existing resistor designs to allow for better, more efficient devices, such as televisions, radios, and computers.

In 1959, Boykin developed his first patent, a wire precision resistor. It was unique in that a person could designate a specific amount of current to fit the purpose of a device. He followed this invention with another patent in 1961 for an inexpensive and easily producible resistor. This improved resistor could also withstand changes in temperature and various shocks without sustaining damage. This second resistor was incredibly popular. Because of Boykin's work, electronic devices could now be made in a more cost-efficient and reliable way. Both consumer markets and the military took advantage of this new ability. Boykin's resistor was used in guided missiles and IBM computers in the United States and other countries. IBM was able to make smaller and faster machines because of the components that Boykin invented.

Boykin is best known for his work on pacemakers. He enabled control functions on the devices, making them the first successful, implantable pacemakers. Pacemakers can help treat people with abnormal heart conditions and those recovering from heart attacks. The devices use electrical impulses to stimulate the heart and encourage a steady heartbeat. Because of Boykin's work, thousands of people with pacemakers are able to extend their lifespans today.

Boykin continued to serve as a consultant throughout the rest of his life, both in the U.S. and Paris. He moved to Paris in 1964, hoping to target the European market there. He worked on many different types of resistors, improving upon his designs. In 1965, he created an electrical capacitor, which is a component that can store electric charge. Two years later, he created an electrical resistance capacitor. He also invented a burglar-proof cash register and a chemical air filter.

Unfortunately, in his later years Boykin had heart problems that his own pacemakers could not address. In 1982, he died of heart failure.

Today Boykin is not as well known as other inventors. This may have to do with his background; as a Black man in the 20th century, his inventions and success may have gone unnoticed and unshared by a more prejudiced society. Boykin grew up in a time of segregated schooling, in which Black and White students were not encouraged to work together and Black students often did not receive the opportunities they deserved. In addition, the Civil Rights Movement did not take place until later on in Boykin's career, meaning that he probably dealt with issues of racism and inequality throughout his life.

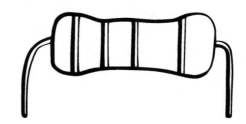

In the past few years, however, more people have rediscovered his impact and are bringing it to light. Today he stands as an example of quiet determination and perseverance in difficult situations. Although he had very little help and could not afford a master's degree, he managed to pursue his inventions and spur the development of computer technology.

References

Bridges, K. (2017). Texas history minute: Boykin's work changed industry, saved lives. *Herald Democrat*. Retrieved from http://www.heralddemocrat.com/news/20170227/boykin8217s-work-changed-industry-saved-lives

Chamberlain, G. (2012). Otis Boykin. *The Black Inventor Online Museum*. Retrieved from http://blackinventor.com/otis-boykin

Massachusetts Institute of Technology. (n.d.). *Otis Boykin*. Retrieved from http://lemelson.mit.edu/resources/otis-boykin

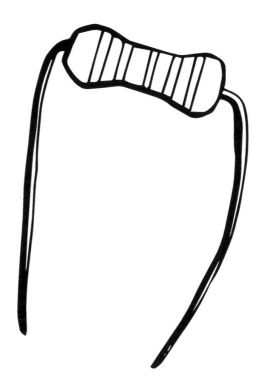

Facing Adversity and Challenges

F3

In what ways have you experienced diminished expectations, lack of opportunity, discrimination, or other adversity beyond your control? Describe how it made you feel. How did you cope with it? Write an essay to reflect on how adversity may be viewed and addressed in positive ways.

Analyzing Adverse Situations and Conditions

F2

How might lack of financial supports and racial discrimination have affected Boykin's career? What evidence supports your response? What aspects of his adversity were within his control? Which ones were beyond his control? Make a generalization about Boykin's adversity, based on your responses.

OTIS BOYKIN

Recognizing Adversity and Challenge

F1

What adversities did Boykin face? Make a list.

Reflecting on Patterns of Achievement

K3

Many people believe that "talent wills out," meaning that if you are talented enough, then you will do well in life. Others believe that "no one ever makes it on their own, that other people are always responsible for one's success." Write an argument that supports one of these views, using Boykin's life story as one of your examples.

Assessing Strengths and Interests

K2

What assets did Boykin possess? How did he use them to his advantage? Write a short essay about how you might use your assets to your advantage.

Identifying Barriers to Achievement

K1

What words and phrases come to mind to describe the barriers that Boykin may have faced? Make a list.

OTIS BOYKIN

Stress Is Not the Enemy

Hi! I'm Mikayla, I'm a competitive swimmer, and I know exactly what it's like to be stressed out! When I was 8 years old, I started swimming competitively with a local club team. Day after day I went to practice, determined to learn more, swim harder, be better. My coaches told me that I had great form. They said that if I worked hard, I could get ranked nationally. I believed them.

I competed in my first swim meet 4 months later. It was so much fun. My team and I—we were like a family. Everyone cheered each other on, screaming from the sidelines and encouraging each other just before our events. The crowd was loud. It all felt exhilarating to me.

My coach had signed me up for two events, a 25-meter freestyle and a 50-meter freestyle. I remember what it felt like on the blocks waiting for the race to begin: the way my heart started to pound and my throat began to close. I remember feeling like I was going to pass out at any minute. The feelings only lasted a second or two before the referee blew the whistle and started the race.

The minute I hit the water, everything else drifted away. I didn't notice my pounding heart or my closing throat. All I heard, all I felt, was the excitement of the race. I had found my bliss.

One day, about 4 years after my first swim meet, my coach talked to me about Junior Olympics. She explained that being in JO was a big honor, and with work and dedication I could likely meet the time requirements to compete. It had been my dream to compete at that level, to one day even be in the Olympic games. I asked my coach to push me harder and harder in practice. I begged her to help me meet my time qualifiers.

Finally, I was ready. I entered several swim meets, all with the quest of meeting my time standards for JO. With each meet, the pounding of my heart got louder and louder; my throat closed more and more. And my ability to silence the noise in my head became more and more difficult.

Still I tried each event, determined to make my times. But I wasn't getting faster. Unable to quiet the noises in my head and consumed by an ever-increasing negative voice inside telling me I would never reach my goals, I began to hate swimming.

I missed a couple of practices. I ignored my coaches' suggestions on ways to improve my times. I avoided additional drills, extra opportunities to improve.

My stress continued to grow. Fueled by my current struggles, my brain started viewing the stress as the problem. I blamed my bad times on the stress of school, the pressures of swim practice, and my inability to meet everyone's ridiculous expectations.

The blaming became a self-fulfilling prophecy. The more I talked about the problems of my stress, the worse the stress got. The more I blamed feeling stressed for my inability to improve in the water, the worse my performance became.

Nothing seemed to help. I was ready to give up. After 4 years and 6 months, I was ready to stop swimming completely—the stress just wasn't worth it. I wanted to feel happy again. I wanted a life without the constant feeling of dread every time I got into a pool.

My coach noticed the changes in me, as did my parents. Everyone told me to push past the "fear" they assumed I was feeling. They told me to just swim, the rest would take care of itself.

I tried. I really tried. But their suggestions didn't stop my heart from pounding out of control. Nor did their advice make me excited to swim again. In fact, it seemed the more they tried to encourage me to push past my feelings, the more stressed I became.

I begged my parents to let me stop swimming. They hesitated but agreed to let me quit at the end of the season, as long as I spoke with my coach about everything.

I delayed talking to my coach for as long as I could—it was so hard to admit to her that her faith in me was unfounded. After all, she was the one who thought I would be great. And I was, for a little while.

Finally, I mustered up the courage to tell her I was leaving the team at the end of the season. She asked me to wait to make a decision until after we could talk. A week later, we sat on the pool deck before practice and talked.

"Tell me about what you feel when you swim," Coach said.

I explained about my pounding heart and closing throat. I told her how my mind couldn't focus when I swam anymore. I told her I was miserable.

"What you are describing is one of the ways your body responds to stress," Coach explained. "But there are other ways you respond, too, ways you may not be aware of."

Coach went on to explain that the body is miraculous in how it responds to stressful events. She talked to me about all of the stress hormones and how they fuel the body. And she explained to me how our brains can sometimes react to stress incorrectly, misreading situations as major threats.

Coach asked me to come to practice early throughout the next week so I could learn more about the positive aspects of stress and how my stress could make me a stronger swimmer. She also asked me not to make any decisions until after we'd worked together.

Over the next several weeks, I learned everything I could about stress, our physical and emotional reactions to stress, and how to ensure that we are responding in the most adaptive way possible. I learned that what I think about stress matters. I also learned that I could change what I felt about stress.

I had to work hard to redefine the role of stress in my life. But I did it. I continued to swim. My heart continued to pound before each event, and my throat felt like it was going to close. Now, however, I understood what was really happening—my body was gearing up to meet a challenge. Each heartbeat provided more oxygen to my cells. My throat wasn't constricting, my lungs were drawing deeper breaths in order to best oxygenate my blood. Everything was working in concert to help me do the best I could.

As my ideas about stress began to change, so did my brain's feelings about swimming. The voice in my head started to quiet. I no longer felt damaged or broken. I felt strong.

I eventually did make my JO times. And I recently received a swim scholarship for college. I owe all of this to my coach. She understood that stress wasn't a problem. It was a solution.

Note. From *Letting Go: A Girl's Guide to Breaking Free of Stress and Anxiety* (pp. 37-39), by C. Fonseca, 2017, Waco, TX: Prufrock Press. Copyright 2017 Prufrock Press. Reprinted with permission.

Creating a Plan for Management

J3

Pretend you are Mikayla. What plan would you design to manage your stress? Cite goals, outcomes desired, and the process(es) you would use to reach them.

Applying Stress Control Techniques

J2

What was the advice of her coach regarding her stress? Have you tried such techniques? How successful were they?

Identifying Conditions/Situations That Cause Stress

J1

In your reading, what conditions of competitive swimming were troubling to Mikayla? How do you identify with these conditions in your own life?

STRESS IS NOT THE ENEMY

K3

Reflecting on Patterns of Achievement

Reflect on what the steps are to extraordinary achievement in your talent development area. What commitments need to be made to ensure you make progress toward your goals?

K2

Assessing Strengths and Interests

Identify your strengths in dealing with barriers. How can you use your strengths to overcome obstacles?

Make a table to illustrate how each of your strengths may be seen as a basis for meeting a short-term goal.

Strengths	Short-Term Goal

K1

Identifying Barriers to Achievement

What does Mikayla see as her barriers to achievement?

What do you see as yours? Make a list that prioritizes your top three barriers.

STRESS IS NOT THE ENEMY

Jacqueline Woodson

Jacqueline Woodson is the author of more than 24 books for young adults and children. Her books often depict the thoughts, feelings, and experiences of young Black characters. Throughout her life, Woodson has focused on writing and telling authentic stories, and she hopes to encourage all kinds of students to read and explore literature.

Born in 1963, Woodson spent her early childhood in the South. Her parents separated when she was very young, and she lived with her grandparents in South Carolina, where segregation was still very much a problem. Although she felt safe in her family circle, Woodson experienced the everyday tension between White and Black people that would impact her novels later on.

A few years later, she moved to Manhattan to be with her mother, a single mom who worked full-time. Woodson and her siblings would walk to the library every day after school to do homework and then read. Although she was a very slow reader, Woodson loved reading the same picture books over and over again, feeling that she was connecting to the stories at a deep level. Her mother made sure that Woodson and her siblings always had library cards and books to read in the house; she believed that education was a tool her children could use to move forward in their lives. She also realized that living in the North offered more opportunities for her children than the segregated South.

Woodson was always happiest when she was writing. She wrote on everything—sidewalks, paper bags, binders, shoes. She also enjoyed telling tall tales to shock her friends, but she would often get in trouble for lying and acting out. It wasn't until fifth grade, when Woodson's teacher complimented her on a story she had written, that Woodson realized she could use her love for storytelling on the page, rather than making trouble in the classroom. She began to write stories and win awards, realizing that writing could bring her freedom and opportunities later in life.

Woodson began writing her first book in college. She was the only Black person in her creative writing workshop, but her teacher encouraged her to draw from her experiences. With this directive in mind, she wrote *Last Summer With Maizon*, a book that explores one girl's experiences after the death of her father and separation from her best friend. Woodson's editor and fans enjoyed the book so much that she wrote two more books in the series; at the time, it was the only trilogy of young adult books to focus on girls of color.

Woodson continued writing middle grade fiction, which she felt came most naturally to her. The experiences and feelings of kids ages 8–11 spoke to her clearly, and she seemed to have a knack for exploring that age group. Other books for young adults included *Locomotion* and *Miracle's Boys*, among many others. She also branched out to write picture books for younger children, as well as poetry. Her book *Brown Girl Dreaming*, which won the National Book Award, is an autobiographical novel written in verse, which explores her experience growing up in the 1960s and 1970s in South Carolina and New York.

Woodson has won many awards for her books, including the Newbery Honor Medal, the Coretta Scott King Award, and the Caldecott Medal. From 2015–2017 she served as the Young People's Poet Laureate, and in 2018, she was named National Ambassador for Young People's Literature. In this position she traveled around the U.S. speaking to kids in schools and libraries, as well as juvenile detention centers. She also plans to make visits to schools in the rural South, an area that receives fewer visiting writers. Her hope is to help kids feel empowered and hopeful about their futures by encouraging them to read, not only as a means of escape, but also as an avenue to grow and develop their minds.

Woodson lives in New York City with her family. She writes full-time, describing each book she writes as a journey in understanding her characters and allowing them to flourish. She credits her continuing success to the support she received from her family, fans, and community.

References

Alter, A. (2018). Jacqueline Woodson is named National Ambassador for Young People's Literature. *The New York Times*. Retrieved from https://www.nytimes.com/2018/01/04/books/jacqueline-woodson-is-named-national-ambassador-for-young-peoples-literature.html

The Brown Bookshelf. (n.d.) *Jacqueline Woodson*. Retrieved from https://thebrownbookshelf.com/2009/02/22/jacqueline-woodson

NPR Code Switch. (2014). *Jacqueline Woodson on growing up, coming out and saying hi to strangers*. Retrieved from https://www.npr.org/sections/codeswitch/2014/12/10/369736205/jacqueline-woodson-on-growing-up-coming-out-and-saying-hi-to-strangers

Woodson, J. (2018). *My biography*. Retrieved from http://www.jacqueline-woodson.com/all-about-me/my-biography

Facing Adversity and Challenges

F3

Woodson faced her challenges head-on and became successful as a writer. Make a plan for developing your own writing skills. What are your goals and outcomes? What is a realistic timeline? How can your adversity be used in a way that allows you to advocate for yourself or others in a career you are interested in?

Analyzing Adverse Situations and Conditions

F2

How did Woodson use her familial adversity to her advantage in developing as a writer? What aspects of adversity have you experienced that would allow you to use it positively? Make a chart showing ways to confront adverse conditions, based on Woodson's story and your own experience.

Adversity Faced	Strategies for Addressing It

Recognizing Adversity and Challenge

F1

What aspects of Woodson's biography demonstrate her encounters with adversity? List all of them that you can discern. Which obstacles do you think would be hardest to overcome? Why?

JACQUELINE WOODSON

Reflecting on Patterns of Achievement

K3

Create a philosophy of learning that honors the importance of at least three of the following principles:

- hard work,
- persistence,
- practice,
- risk-taking,
- self-assessment,
- collaborating with others, and
- mindfulness.

Develop your philosophy into a goal-setting plan, discussing the rationale for your top three criteria.

Assessing Strengths and Interests

K2

How did Woodson use learning skills to overcome these barriers? What strengths do you have that allow you to overcome obstacles? Name them and cite how they can assist you in overcoming obstacles.

Identifying Barriers to Achievement

K1

What barriers to achievement did Woodson face? What underlying beliefs and values did she possess that could help her overcome them?

JACQUELINE WOODSON

Lou Gehrig Farewell Speech

Find Lou Gehrig's farewell speech online. It is available in writing on several sites (including http://www.lougehrig.com) and also in audio. Provide background information about Lou Gehrig if students are not familiar with his accomplishments. Explain that he was one of the greatest baseball players of all time. He played more than 2,130 consecutive games. He even played baseball when he had broken bones. He was nicknamed the "Iron Horse" because of his persistence and endurance. He was also a leading home run hitter. Baseball was a significant part of his life until he was diagnosed in 1939 with ALS, a degenerative disease, which is now known as Lou Gehrig's Disease. He died 2 years after this speech was given.

If listening to an audio recording instead of providing the speech in writing, provide specific questions for each ladder rung ahead of time so that subsequent listening sessions allow students to focus on answering specific questions. Additional opportunities for listening to the speech may be provided at a computer center if students are working independently on jotting down responses before discussing their responses in small- or whole-group settings.

Reference

Lougehrig.com. (2018). *Biography*. Retrieved from https://www.lougehrig.com/biography

Facing Adversity and Challenges

How did Lou Gehrig take his adversity and reframe it into something positive? Which specific quotes show this? Think of an adverse situation you are going or have gone through. How might you reframe it in a way that is realistic and not falsely positive or negative? Consider what is in your control and what is not as you reframe it. Write up your reframing of the situation and share with a partner.

Analyzing Adverse Situations and Conditions

How would you analyze Lou Gehrig's situation after he is diagnosed? What is in his control? What is not in his control? What would you say to an ALS patient today if you were his or her doctor, based on your reading about the disease?

Recognizing Adversity and Challenge

What was Lou Gehrig's "bad break"? Conduct a quick search of Lou Gehrig's life and ALS to learn more. People started calling ALS "Lou Gehrig's Disease." This means that at the time of his diagnosis little was known about the disease. How does that fact impact the way you view his speech?

Actualizing Potential to Advance a Goal

H3

How does one focus on a passion and still have an identity outside of his or her work, according to what you can infer from Gehrig's speech and situation? What are the aspects of your identity—think about the roles you have and create a concept map that shows at least five of them (family member, sports team member, Girl Scout, etc.). Now write a short autobiographical sketch that highlights some of your main roles and the emphasis you place on each one.

Understanding Roles and Affiliations

H2

How did Gehrig use his family affiliation as a source of strength? What sources of strength do you have when there are difficult times? With whom or with what do you affiliate? Draw a figure to illustrate your connections and sources of strength.

Knowing Oneself

H1

In what ways does Lou Gehrig show that he understands himself in his speech? How does he describe his identity?

LOU GEHRIG FAREWELL SPEECH

A Happy Life

Show the following the TED Talk video by Sam Berns before asking students to respond to the subsequent ladders:

- My Philosophy for a Happy Life, Sam Berns, TEDxMidAtlantic: https://www.youtube.com/watch?v=36m1o-tM05g

As students watch the video, ask them to think about how Sam Berns handled his adverse situation and assets to achieve his goals and live a happy life. You may also choose to explain that Sam had progeria, a disease in which someone ages at an accelerated pace.

After watching the videos once, provide specific questions for each ladder rung so that subsequent viewings can be targeted toward answering specific questions. Additional opportunities for viewing the video may be provided at a computer center if students are working independently on jotting down responses before discussing in small- or whole-group settings.

Facing Adversity and Challenges

F3

Does experiencing adversity make one stronger? Create a short dialogue or skit between Sam Berns and a book character of your choosing that answers this question from each individual's perspective and provides advice for others to consider. Be sure each individual in your dialogue references specific events, quotes, or situations experienced.

Analyzing Adverse Situations and Conditions

F2

Sam Berns dealt with his adversity in a positive way, even though it was difficult. Why do you think some people deal with adversity in more positive than negative ways? Think about Sam Berns and someone in real life or a book who faced a challenge but handled it poorly. What factors made the biggest difference in responses to a difficult situation and personal success? Create a Venn diagram to show the similarities and differences.

Recognizing Adversity and Challenge

F1

How did Sam Berns's diagnosis of progeria and related health issues contribute to the importance of his message and outlook on life? Explain.

A HAPPY LIFE

Reflecting on Patterns of Achievement

K3

Revisit Sam Berns's philosophy for having a happy life as outlined and shown on the slide at the end of his talk. How does his philosophy align with yours? Design your own recipe for a happy life that includes your definition of happiness and provides at least four specific points about the relationship between happiness and achieving one's goals. How do the "ingredients" in your recipe interact to create a positive situation?

Assessing Strengths and Interests

K2

You may have heard the popular saying, "If life gives you lemons, make lemonade." How did Sam Berns make lemonade? Make a list of specific assets (personal and external) he used. How did those assets help him reach his goals?

Identifying Barriers to Achievement

K1

How did Sam Berns view the barriers he faced in life? Create a list of quotes from his speech that answers this question. Compare your quotes with those of a classmate. Select just one quote from your and your classmate's collective lists that best exemplifies how someone should view his or her barriers to success; discuss why your selected quote is the most appropriate. (Select a quote other than one of the four bullet points at the conclusion of the video.)

Pre- and Postassessments, Rubric, and Discussion Checklist

Appendix A contains the pre- and postassessment readings and questions, as well as a rubric for scoring the assessments. The preassessment should be administered before any work with *Jacob's Ladder* is conducted. After the readings and ladders have been completed, or midway through the program, the postassessment can be given to track student improvement on the ladder skill sets or to continue to guide targeted activities.

Appendix A also includes a discussion checklist that teachers may use to analyze whether or not students understand key content through group or individual responses that may not be in writing.

Preassessment

Oprah Winfrey

Oprah Winfrey is a television pioneer, producer, actress, and philanthropist whose long-running talk show inspired millions of viewers. Her warm personality and dedicated outreach allowed her to become one of the wealthiest and most influential Black women alive today. She also has inspired many children and adults to read well-crafted books through her Oprah Book Club selections that have been promoted worldwide.

Winfrey was born in rural Mississippi in 1954. Her parents were not married and separated not too long after her birth. Her grandmother took care of her through the age of 2, which was also when Oprah's grandmother taught her to read. When Oprah started kindergarten, she wrote a note to her teacher saying she was better suited for first grade and she was moved. She was later moved to third grade because of her ability to learn things quickly and with depth.

During Oprah's elementary and early adolescent years she transitioned between her mother's and father's homes a few times. Living with her mother in Milwaukee, WI, proved to be a difficult time for Oprah, as she lived in an unsafe and poor area of the city and also suffered abuse by various male family members and friends of her mother. Oprah's quality of life improved greatly, however, when she moved to Nashville, TN, to live with her father, a barber and businessman. He proved to be a positive influence on her emotional development, and Winfrey gained confidence that she would carry with her into her career. Oprah's father prioritized education. She was required to write weekly book reports and show that she learned at least five new vocabulary words each night at dinner. She loved giving speeches and had opportunities to speak at several gatherings. She once received $500 for a speech she gave and decided at that moment that she enjoyed speaking and wanted a career where she was paid to talk.

In high school, Winfrey gained her first experience in the media industry, working at a Nashville radio station, reading the afternoon news. She was also involved in several school clubs and was an excellent student. She earned a full scholarship to Tennessee State University where she continued to pursue her interest in media and television. At 19, she became the first female African American anchor on a CBS affiliate news program in Nashville, while she was still a sophomore in college. Although the experience helped her grow professionally, she also felt limited by the objectivity required from this type of journalism.

In 1976, Winfrey moved to Baltimore, MD, to host a morning TV chat show, *People Are Talking*. Her engaging and warm approach to the role quickly gained viewers, as well as the attention of media executives. She was soon recruited by a Chicago station to host *A.M. Chicago*, a program that was struggling with viewership. Winfrey transformed the show with her honest and open personality and the discussion of debatable and current issues instead of the more traditional focus on cooking, clothing, and housekeeping. The program earned first-place ratings in just a few months. The program was renamed *The Oprah Winfrey Show* and was nationally syndicated in 1986, reaching viewers across the U.S. It grossed $125 million in its first year with an audience of 10 million. Winfrey soon gained ownership of the show, placing it under Harpo Productions, her new production company. *The Oprah Winfrey Show* ran until 2011, receiving several Emmy Awards and appearing in more than 100 countries worldwide. At its height, it had grown to an audience of 40 million viewers a week.

Winfrey also appeared in dramatic roles in film and television. Her first role was in Steven Spielberg's movie *The Color Purple* in 1985. She received an Academy Award nomination for Best Supporting Actress for her performance. She later lent her vocal talents to several animated movies, appeared in television movies and miniseries, such as *The Women of Brewster Place*, and had roles in blockbusters, such as *A Wrinkle in Time*. Winfrey's roles often depicted strong African American women navigating difficult circumstances. As a producer, Winfrey made depicting Black stories a key goal, bringing acclaimed novels such as *Their Eyes Were Watching God* and *Beloved* to television and thereby sharing those stories with a wider audience. In 2005, Winfrey became a producer of the musical *The Color Purple* on Broadway. She would later coproduce a revival of the musical in 2015, which would receive a Tony Award.

Winfrey's other accomplishments included the launching of Oprah's Book Club, an on-air book club that revitalized pleasure reading and brought unknown authors to the forefront; Oxygen Media, a cable and Internet company directed toward women; and *O: Oprah Magazine*, a lifestyle magazine. After *The Oprah Winfrey Show* ended, Winfrey moved to her own network, OWN (the Oprah Winfrey Network). The network had trouble gaining viewers initially, but Winfrey persevered until her programming gained attention once more.

Winfrey is a great philanthropist, using her vast wealth and resources to target issues that are meaningful to her. She even proposed a bill to Congress that would protect children from abusers. The bill, signed into law in 1993, became the National Child Protection Act. Oprah's Angel Network has also raised more than $50 million for charity. Some of the projects included helping girls pursue education in South Africa and bringing relief to victims of Hurricane Katrina. The Oprah Winfrey Foundation is a charity that offers support to women and families around the world.

Winfrey has received many awards and recognition for her charitable work. In 2002, she became the first recipient of the Bob Hope Humanitarian Award. In 2013, Winfrey received the Presidential Medal of Freedom, and in 2018, she became the first Black woman at the Golden Globes to receive the Cecil B. DeMille Award for lifetime achievement.

Throughout her life, Winfrey has used her openhearted personality to inspire viewers, create new programming and narratives for strong Black women, and support philanthropy across the world. She continues to use her influence today for positive ends.

References

Biography.com. (2018). *Oprah Winfrey biography*. https://www.biography.com/people/oprah-winfrey-9534419

Encyclopedia Britannica. (2018). *Oprah Winfrey*. Retrieved from https://www.britannica.com/biography/Oprah-Winfrey

Oprah.com. (2017). *Oprah Winfrey's official biography*. Retrieved from http://www.oprah.com/pressroom/oprah-winfreys-official-biography/1

Encyclopedia of World Biography. (2018). *Oprah Winfrey Biography*. Retrieved from http://www.notablebiographies.com/We-Z/Winfrey-Oprah.html

Preassessment: Questions

Read and answer each question, using evidence from the reading to support your ideas.

1. What personal qualities contributed to Winfrey's success? Identify at least three and explain why these qualities are important to possess.

_____

_____

_____

_____

_____

_____

_____

2. What strategies did or might Winfrey have used to overcome barriers to success? Explain the hardships Winfrey faced and at least two ways she successfully addressed or could have addressed these hardships in a way that positively contributed to her success. Consider both personal and external hardships.

_____

_____

_____

_____

_____

_____

_____

Preassessment: Questions, *continued.*

3. How does one's identity, family, perceptions of self and others, environment, education, and/or experience shape one's future? Select at least two of these factors that you view most important in influencing one's future and explain why.

_____

_____

_____

_____

_____

_____

_____

4. What symbol best describes the theme of Winfrey's life? Explain how the symbol you selected represented one of Winfrey's life themes.

_____

_____

_____

_____

_____

_____

_____

Postassessment

Warren Buffett

Warren Buffett, also known as the "Oracle of Omaha," is one of the most successful and wealthiest investors of all time. Born in Nebraska in 1930, he began building his fortune at age 11 when he bought stock for the first time. Today, his net worth is estimated at around $84 billion. Although his great success was met with setbacks, obstacles did not stop him from becoming one of the most respected businessmen and generous philanthropists in the world.

Buffett's father was a stockbroker and a U.S. congressman, and his mother was a homemaker. From an early age, Buffett demonstrated mathematics and financial skills. As well as investing in the stock market as a child, he had three profitable businesses in his teenage years. He ran a successful newspaper delivery route, sold horseracing tip sheets, and, later, owned three pinball machines installed in three different locations. By 16, he had earned more than $53,000 and had enrolled at the University of Pennsylvania to study business. Two years later, he transferred to the University of Nebraska and soon graduated at age 20 with a bachelor's degree in business administration.

He then applied to Harvard Business School—and was rejected. "Forget it," the staff said during an admissions interview, "You're not going to Harvard." Although disappointed, Buffett learned that Benjamin Graham, the author of *The Intelligent Investor* and the "father of value investing," taught at Columbia Business School. Buffett applied, was accepted and enrolled at Columbia, earning his master's degree by 1951.

That year, as he started a job as an investment salesman, he proposed to his future wife, Susan Thompson. Buffett's father-in-law invited him for a chat. "You're going to fail," Buffett later recalled his father-in-law saying of his career path. But his future father-in-law was wrong.

From 1951 to 1956, Buffett worked as an investment salesman and then as a securities analyst. He founded his own investment partnership in 1956, and, because he was very skilled at identifying undervalued companies, became a millionaire. He began accumulating stock of one such company, Berkshire Hathaway, in the early 1960s, and by 1965 he took over the company. The company, which focused on textiles, wasn't performing as well as it could. Thus, he greatly expanded it, focusing on the insurance sector and then moving into other industries. Berkshire Hathaway now owns Geico, Duracell, Dairy Queen, and more. It also has minority interest in major companies like Kraft Heinz, American Express, and Coca-Cola.

Buffett first became a billionaire in the 1990s. When he was 52, Buffet's net worth was $376 million. But after turning 60 in 1990, he was worth more than $3.8 billion. Surprisingly, he has earned about 94% of his wealth since turning 60. By the end of 2013, his net worth was close to $59 billion, and, thanks to rising stock prices, he was earning $37 million a day. Despite his great wealth, he still uses a Nokia flip phone, and he has lived in the same house for 60 years—a relatively modest two-story home in Omaha, NE, that he purchased for $31,500 in 1958—with his wife and three children.

In an interview with *Fortune* magazine, Buffett once said he intended to leave his three children "enough money so that they would feel they could do anything, but not so much that they could do nothing." Throughout the years, when called ungenerous with his wealth, he argued that it was better if he continued to earn more until he passed away, so that as much money could be given away as possible. Something changed, however. No one knows why—perhaps because of age or because of his wife passing away in 2004—but, in 2006, Buffett pledged to give away most of his fortune during his lifetime.

He committed 85% of his wealth ($37 billion at the time) to the Bill and Melinda Gates Foundation. The foundation, started by Microsoft founder and Buffett's friend, Bill Gates, is dedicated to improving health and education in poor nations. The pledge to the organization was the largest philanthropic donation in history. With Gates, Buffett later formed The Giving Pledge campaign in 2010 to encourage more wealthy individuals to give money to good causes. Buffett also gave shares worth $1 billion to each of his three children—Susan, Peter, and Howard—who each run their own philanthropic organizations. In 2012, Buffett pledged an additional 12 million shares to his children (about $2.5 billion each), making them some of the world's most powerful philanthropists. Susan works to improve the lives of children in Nebraska through the Sherwood Foundation and supports affordable women's healthcare through the Susan Thompson Buffett Foundation. Peter works to help girls living in poverty through the NoVo Foundation. Meanwhile, Howard seeks to end world hunger through the Howard G. Buffett Foundation.

Susan, Peter, and Howard have all seen successes because Buffett encouraged them not to fear failure. "I've told them that unless they had failures, they *were* failures," he told *The Atlantic* in 2016. "It's the nature of philanthropy—that you're going to fail. In business, I'm looking for the easy pitches. . . . Philanthropy is just the opposite. You're dealing with problems that are huge and that have resisted easy solutions."

Buffett was diagnosed and underwent successful treatment for prostate cancer in 2012, but the illness did not hold him up for long. Today, he continues to grow Berkshire Hathaway and pursue other causes. In 2016, he launched Drive2Vote, an organization to support Nebraska voters, and he was a vocal Democratic supporter in the 2016 election. Then, in early 2018, Berkshire Hathaway, JPMorgan Chase, and Amazon announced they were planning to work together to form a new healthcare company for employees. Buffett said of the partnership, "We share the belief that putting our collective resources behind the country's best talent can, in time, check the rise in health costs while concurrently enhancing patient satisfaction and outcomes."

When he started at age 11, few could have guessed that Warren Buffett would become one of the wealthiest people in the world, but his hard work and careful attention to the lessons of failure over the course of more than seven decades have helped him not only grow his fortune, but also influence many other businessman, investors, and philanthropists.

References

Biography.com. (2018). *Warren Buffett biography*. Retrieved from https://www.biography.com/people/warren-buffett-9230729

Forbes. (2018). *Warren Buffett*. Retrieved from https://www.forbes.com/profile/warren-buffett

Leadem, R. (2018). 25 surprising facts about Warren Buffett. *Entrepreneur*. Retrieved from https://www.entrepreneur.com/article/290381

Munk, N. (2016). How Warren Buffet's son would feed the world. *The Atlantic*. Retrieved from https://www.theatlantic.com/magazine/archive/2016/05/how-warren-buffetts-son-would-feed-the-world/476385

O'Brien, T. L., & Saul, S. (2006). Buffett to give bulk of his fortune to Gates charity. *The New York Times*. Retrieved from https://www.nytimes.com/2006/06/26/business/26buffett.html

Postassessment: Questions

Read and answer each question, using evidence from the reading to support your ideas.

1. What personal qualities contributed to Buffett's success? Identify at least three and explain why these qualities are important to possess.

    _____

    _____

    _____

    _____

    _____

    _____

    _____

2. What strategies did or might Buffett have used to overcome barriers to success? Explain the hardships Buffett faced and at least two ways he successfully addressed or could have addressed these hardships in a way that positively contributed to his success. Consider both personal and external hardships.

    _____

    _____

    _____

    _____

    _____

    _____

    _____

Postassessment: Questions, *continued.*

3. How does one's identity, family, perceptions of self and others, environment, education, and/or experience shape one's future? Select at least two of these factors that you view most important in influencing one's future and explain why.

_____

_____

_____

_____

_____

_____

_____

_____

4. What symbol best describes the theme of Buffett's life? Explain how the symbol you selected represented one of Buffett's life themes.

_____

_____

_____

_____

_____

_____

_____

_____

Rubric for Scoring the Pre- and Postassessments

4 = Highly Effective   3 = Effective   2 = Somewhat Effective   1 = Not Effective

Question	Points				
	0	1	2	3	4
1 **Attributes for Success (Developing Excellence)**	Provides no response or response is inappropriate to the task demand.	Limited; only lists two characteristics and limited to no evidence.	Response includes at least three accurate characteristics but does not include why the characteristics are important to possess or includes limited or irrelevant evidence.	Response includes at least three accurate characteristics that are important to possess and includes accurate evidence from the biography regarding why these are important to possess.	Response includes at least three characteristics that are important for success and provides substantial and relevant evidence from the biography about why these are important to possess.
2 **Barriers and Strategies to Overcome (Coping With Adversity)**	Provides no response or response is inappropriate to the task demand.	Limited, vague, inaccurate response; or does not address all parts of the question.	Response addresses all parts of the question; barriers, strategies, and personal applications are not fully supported and/or substantial.	Response addresses all parts of the question; barriers, strategies, and personal applications are provided and supported with personal and textual evidence.	Response addresses all parts of the question; barriers, strategies, and personal applications show unique insights and connections to each other; ideas are supported with personal and textual evidence.
3 **Factors for Success (Identity)**	Provides no response or response is inappropriate to the task demand.	Limited, vague, inaccurate response; does not address all parts of the question.	Accurate response; addresses all parts of the question; does not connect the two most important factors chosen to the biography or does not provide adequate support for why the selected factors are most important to one's identity.	Insightful response; addresses all parts of the question; connects the two most important factors chosen to the biography and provides support for why the selected factors are important to one's identity.	Insightful response; addresses all parts of the question; connects the two most important factors chosen to the biography and provides a convincing rationale for how the factors are related to one's identity.
Life Themes and Symbols (Multiple Ladders, Depending Upon the Theme Chosen)	Provides no response or response is inappropriate to the task demand.	Provides a response that is inaccurate or is not a symbol; provides a symbol but inaccurate life theme.	Provides a symbol that is relevant and connects to an inconsequential life theme; rationale or connection to the biography is missing or limited.	Provides a symbol that is relevant and connects to an important life theme; rationale or connection to the biography is explained with evidence.	Provides a symbol that explains an important and substantial life theme and includes detailed information about how the symbol and theme is represented throughout the course of the person's life.

Discussion Checklist: A Guide for Monitoring Student Talk

1 = rarely   2 = sometimes   3 = most of the time

The student:	1	2	3
a. Provides evidence from the text or personal experiences (when appropriate) to support ideas without being prompted.			
b. Contributes to discussions by asking questions of other students.			
c. Self-monitors comments and communications. Does not dominate discussions or overshare.			
d. Waits his or her turn for talking without interrupting others.			
e. Comes prepared to discuss ideas in a group, positively contributing to the conversation.			
f. Is respectful of all group members' ideas—even if they disagree.			
g. Asks other students for evidence before making a judgment. Disagrees with ideas and not students.			
h. Stays on topic. Uses discussion prompts to promote instead of stifle conversation.			
i. Clearly articulates ideas in an understandable and concise way.			
j. Honors pre-established group norms for discussions both in and out of the classroom.			
k. Uses appropriate nonverbal language when engaging in the discussion.			
Teacher Evidence of Student Progress:			

APPENDIX

B

Classroom Diagnostic Forms

Appendix B contains classroom diagnostic forms. These forms are for teachers and are designed to aid them in keeping track of the progress and skill mastery of their students. With these charts, teachers can record student progress in relation to each ladder skill within a genre and select additional ladders and readings based on student needs.

Classroom Diagnostic Form

Short Stories and Media

Use this document to record student completion of ladder sets with the assessment of work.

0 = Needs More Practice With the Given Skill Set   1 = Understands and Applies Skills   2 = Applies Skills Very Effectively

Student Name	The Man, the Boy, and the Donkey		Wonder Trailer		Music		Eleven		The Leaping Match		Geri's Game		The Four Crafts-Men		Piper	
	F	H	G	I	G	J	E	H	G	I	G	I	I	K	F	G

Classroom Diagnostic Form

Poetry

Use this document to record student completion of ladder sets with the assessment of work.

0 = Needs More Practice With the Given Skill Set   1 = Understands and Applies Skills   2 = Applies Skills Very Effectively

Student Name	Success Is Counted Sweeter		Mending		The Fool's Song		Casey at the Bat		A Lazy Day		Winter Branches	From a Bridge Car
	K	L	K	L	E	J	J	L	E	J	E	E

Classroom Diagnostic Form

Biographies, Essays, and Speeches

Use this document to record student completion of ladder sets with the assessment of work.

0 = Needs More Practice With the Given Skill Set   1 = Understands and Applies Skills   2 = Applies Skills Very Effectively

Student Name	Engineers: Failures and Success		The Buddy Bench		A Literary Lesson on Making Mistakes		Girls in STEM		Otis Boykin		Stress Is Not the Enemy		Jacqueline Woodson		Lou Gehrig Farewell Speech		A Happy Life	
	G	L	E	F	G	J	G	K	F	K	J	K	F	K	F	H	F	K

About the Authors

Joyce VanTassel-Baska, Ed.D., is the Jody and Layton Smith Professor Emerita of Education and former Executive Director of the Center for Gifted Education at William & Mary in Virginia, where she developed a graduate program and a research and development center in gifted education. She also initiated and directed the Center for Talent Development at Northwestern University. Prior to her work in higher education, Dr. VanTassel-Baska served as the state director of gifted programs for Illinois, as a regional director of a gifted service center in the Chicago area, as coordinator of gifted programs for the Toledo, OH, public school system, and as a teacher of gifted high school students in English and Latin. She is past president of The Association for the Gifted of the Council for Exceptional Children, the Northwestern University Chapter of Phi Delta Kappa, and the National Association for Gifted Children.

Dr. VanTassel-Baska has published widely, including 27 books and more than 500 refereed journal articles, book chapters, and scholarly reports. Recent books include: *Content-Based Curriculum for High-Ability Learners* (3rd ed., 2017, with Catherine Little), *Patterns and Profiles of Promising Learners From Poverty* (2010), and *Social-Emotional Curriculum With Gifted and Talented Students* (2009, with Tracy Cross and Rick Olenchak). She also served as the editor of *Gifted and Talented International,* a publication of the World Council on Gifted and Talented, for 7 years from 1998–2005.

Tamra Stambaugh, Ph.D., is an assistant research professor in special education and executive director of Programs for Talented Youth at Vanderbilt University. Stambaugh conducts research in gifted education with a focus on students living in rural settings, students of poverty, and curriculum and instructional interventions that promote gifted student learning. She is the coauthor/coeditor of several books including *Comprehensive Curriculum for Gifted Learners* (2007, with Joyce VanTassel-Baska), *Overlooked Gems: A National Perspective on Low-Income Promising Students* (2007, with Joyce VanTassel-Baska), *Leading Change in Gifted Education* (2009, with Bronwyn MacFarlane), the *Jacob's Ladder Reading Comprehension Program Series* (2008, 2009, 2010, 2011, 2012, 2016, with Joyce VanTassel-Baska), *Effective Curriculum for Underserved Gifted Students* (2012, with Kim Chandler), *Serving Gifted Students in Rural Settings* (TAGT Legacy Book Award Winner, with Susannah Wood), and Advanced Curriculum From Vanderbilt University's Programs for Talented Youth series (2016, with Emily Mofield). Stambaugh has also written numerous articles and book chapters. She frequently provides keynotes, professional development workshops, and consultation to school districts nationally and internationally and shares her work at refereed research conferences.

Stambaugh is the recipient of several awards, including the Margaret The Lady Thatcher Medallion for scholarship, service, and character from the William & Mary School of Education; the Doctoral Student Award, Early Leader Award, and several curriculum awards from the National Association for Gifted Children; the Jo Patterson Service Award and Curriculum Award from the Tennessee Association for Gifted Children; and the Higher Education Award from the Ohio Association for Gifted Children. Stambaugh has received or directed research and service grants totaling over $7.5 million. Prior to her appointment at Vanderbilt she was director of grants and special projects at William & Mary's Center for Gifted Education, where she earned her Ph.D.

Common Core
State Standards

The *Affective Jacob's Ladder Series* uses literature, media, biography, and other resources as a springboard for focusing on affective needs of gifted learners. Within this framework, standards-based English language arts process skills can also be addressed and practiced in tandem with affective goals. For example, students may discuss coping strategies, feelings, reactions, or ideas about a particular situation as prompted by a character's approach to a problem, the theme or plot of a text, how a famous person dealt with adversity and success, or how writing can be a therapeutic way to convey thoughts and feelings. Successful class discussions and responses to ladder questions rely upon a students' understanding of a resource prompt, the use of evidence to support ideas, writing in a way that effectively conveys ideas and emotions, and practicing speaking and listening strategies. Thus, dependent upon the ladder focus and resource used, the following Common Core State Standards may be seen as links to the social-emotional learning outcomes of the program.

Standard: Reading Literature	Grade 4	Grade 5
CCSS.ELA-LITERACY.RL.4.1 OR CCSS.ELA-LITERACY.RL.5.1	Refer to details and examples in a text when explaining what the text says explicitly and when drawing inferences from the text.	Quote accurately from a text when explaining what the text says explicitly and when drawing inferences from the text.
CCSS.ELA-LITERACY.RL.4.2 OR CCSS.ELA-LITERACY.RL.5.2	Determine a theme of a story, drama, or poem from details in the text; summarize the text.	Determine a theme of a story, drama, or poem from details in the text, including how characters in a story or drama respond to challenges or how the speaker in a poem reflects upon a topic; summarize the text.
CCSS.ELA-LITERACY.RL.4.3 OR CCSS.ELA-LITERACY.RL.5.3	Describe in depth a character, setting, or event in a story or drama, drawing on specific details in the text (e.g., a character's thoughts, words, or actions).	Compare and contrast two or more characters, settings, or events in a story or drama, drawing on specific details in the text (e.g., how characters interact).
CCSS.ELA-LITERACY.RL.4.4 OR CCSS.ELA-LITERACY.RL.5.4	Determine the meaning of words and phrases as they are used in a text, including those that allude to significant characters found in mythology (e.g., Herculean).	Determine the meaning of words and phrases as they are used in a text, including figurative language such as metaphors and similes.
CCSS.ELA-LITERACY.RL.4.6 OR CCSS.ELA-LITERACY.RL.5.6		Describe how a narrator's or speaker's point of view influences how events are described.

Standard: Reading Informational Text	Grade 4	Grade 5
CCSS.ELA-LITERACY.RI.4.1 OR CCSS.ELA-LITERACY.RI.5.1	Refer to details and examples in a text when explaining what the text says explicitly and when drawing inferences from the text.	Quote accurately from a text when explaining what the text says explicitly and when drawing inferences from the text.

Standard: Reading Informational Text, continued.	Grade 4, continued.	Grade 5, continued.
CCSS.ELA-LITERACY.RI.4.3 OR CCSS.ELA-LITERACY.RI.5.3	Explain events, procedures, ideas, or concepts in a historical, scientific, or technical text, including what happened and why, based on specific information in the text.	Explain the relationships or interactions between two or more individuals, events, ideas, or concepts in a historical, scientific, or technical text based on specific information in the text.
CCSS.ELA-LITERACY.RI.4.8 OR CCSS.ELA-LITERACY.RI.5.8	Explain how an author uses reasons and evidence to support particular points in a text.	Explain how an author uses reasons and evidence to support particular points in a text, identifying which reasons and evidence support which point(s).

Standard: Writing	Grade 4	Grade 5
CCSS.ELA-LITERACY.W.4.1 OR CCSS.ELA-LITERACY.W.5.1	Write opinion pieces on topics or texts, supporting a point of view with reasons and information.	Write opinion pieces on topics or texts, supporting a point of view with reasons and information.
CCSS.ELA-LITERACY.W.4.1.A OR CCSS.ELA-LITERACY.W.5.1.A	Introduce a topic or text clearly, state an opinion, and create an organizational structure in which related ideas are grouped to support the writer's purpose.	Introduce a topic or text clearly, state an opinion, and create an organizational structure in which ideas are logically grouped to support the writer's purpose.
CCSS.ELA-LITERACY.W.4.1.B OR CCSS.ELA-LITERACY.W.5.1.B	Provide reasons that are supported by facts and details.	Provide logically ordered reasons that are supported by facts and details.
CCSS.ELA-LITERACY.W.4.1.D OR CCSS.ELA-LITERACY.W.5.1.D	Provide a concluding statement or section related to the opinion presented.	Provide a concluding statement or section related to the opinion presented.

Standard: Writing, continued.	Grade 4, continued.	Grade 5, continued.
CCSS.ELA-LITERACY.W.4.2 OR CCSS.ELA-LITERACY.W.5.2	Write informative/explanatory texts to examine a topic and convey ideas and information clearly.	Write informative/explanatory texts to examine a topic and convey ideas and information clearly.
CCSS.ELA-LITERACY.W.4.2.B OR CCSS.ELA-LITERACY.W.5.2.B	Develop the topic with facts, definitions, concrete details, quotations, or other information and examples related to the topic.	Develop the topic with facts, definitions, concrete details, quotations, or other information and examples related to the topic.
CCSS.ELA-LITERACY.W.4.3 OR CCSS.ELA-LITERACY.W.5.3	Write narratives to develop real or imagined experiences or events using effective technique, descriptive details, and clear event sequences.	Write narratives to develop real or imagined experiences or events using effective technique, descriptive details, and clear event sequences.
CCSS.ELA-LITERACY.W.4.3.B OR CCSS.ELA-LITERACY.W.5.3.B	Use dialogue and description to develop experiences and events or show the responses of characters to situations.	Use narrative techniques, such as dialogue, description, and pacing, to develop experiences and events or show the responses of characters to situations.
CCSS.ELA-LITERACY.W.4.3.D OR CCSS.ELA-LITERACY.W.5.3.D	Use concrete words and phrases and sensory details to convey experiences and events precisely.	Use concrete words and phrases and sensory details to convey experiences and events precisely.
CCSS.ELA-LITERACY.W.4.3.E OR CCSS.ELA-LITERACY.W.5.3.E	Provide a conclusion that follows from the narrated experiences or events.	Provide a conclusion that follows from the narrated experiences or events.

Standard: Writing, continued.	Grade 4, continued.	Grade 5, continued.
CCSS.ELA-LITERACY.W.4.4 OR CCSS.ELA-LITERACY.W.5.4	Produce clear and coherent writing in which the development and organization are appropriate to task, purpose, and audience. (Grade-specific expectations for writing types are defined in standards 1–3 above.)	Produce clear and coherent writing in which the development and organization are appropriate to task, purpose, and audience. (Grade-specific expectations for writing types are defined in standards 1–3 above.)
CCSS.ELA-LITERACY.W.4.8 OR CCSS.ELA-LITERACY.W.5.8	Recall relevant information from experiences or gather relevant information from print and digital sources; (The second part of the standard is deleted, as it is not applicable).	Recall relevant information from experiences or gather relevant information from print and digital sources; (The second part of standard is deleted, as it is not applicable).
CCSS.ELA-LITERACY.W.4.9 OR CCSS.ELA-LITERACY.W.5.9	Draw evidence from literary or informational texts to support analysis, reflection, and research.	Draw evidence from literary or informational texts to support analysis, reflection, and research.

Standard: Speaking and Listening	Grade 4	Grade 5
CCSS.ELA-LITERACY.SL.4.1 OR CCSS.ELA-LITERACY.SL.5.1	Engage effectively in a range of collaborative discussions (one-on-one, in groups, and teacher-led) with diverse partners on grade 4 topics and texts, building on others' ideas and expressing their own clearly.	Engage effectively in a range of collaborative discussions (one-on-one, in groups, and teacher-led) with diverse partners on grade 5 topics and texts, building on others' ideas and expressing their own clearly.
CCSS.ELA-LITERACY.SL.4.1.A OR CCSS.ELA-LITERACY.SL.5.1.A	Come to discussions prepared, having read or studied required material; explicitly draw on that preparation and other information known about the topic to explore ideas under discussion.	Come to discussions prepared, having read or studied required material; explicitly draw on that preparation and other information known about the topic to explore ideas under discussion.

Standard: Speaking and Listening, continued.	Grade 4, continued.	Grade 5, continued.
CCSS.ELA-LITERACY.SL.4.1.B OR CCSS.ELA-LITERACY.SL.5.1.B	Follow agreed-upon rules for discussions and carry out assigned roles.	Follow agreed-upon rules for discussions and carry out assigned roles.
CCSS.ELA-LITERACY.SL.4.1.C OR CCSS.ELA-LITERACY.SL.5.1.C	Pose and respond to specific questions to clarify or follow up on information, and make comments that contribute to the discussion and link to the remarks of others.	Pose and respond to specific questions by making comments that contribute to the discussion and elaborate on the remarks of others.
CCSS.ELA-LITERACY.SL.4.1.D OR CCSS.ELA-LITERACY.SL.5.1.D	Review the key ideas expressed and explain their own ideas and understanding in light of the discussion.	Review the key ideas expressed and draw conclusions in light of information and knowledge gained from the discussions.

Alignment to the NAGC Program Standards

Several of the National Association for Gifted Children professional program standards in gifted education address the areas selected for emphasis in the *Affective Jacob's Ladder Reading Comprehension Program*. Below are the relevant standards within the categories of Learning and Development (Standard 1), Curriculum Planning and Instruction (Standard 3) and Learning Environments (Standard 4) that may prove useful in aligning the work that gifted learners are performing through *Affective Jacob's Ladder* to professional standards in the field. These standards include outcomes for students and ways educators can encourage these outcomes in their instruction and professional practice.

The standards outlined below focus specifically on learning areas important to the affective development of gifted learners and the opportunities the *Affective Jacob's Ladder* curriculum may provide, depending upon the teacher's pedagogical approach and specific ladder questions. Other skill sets have also been included as cognitive learning works in tandem with affective development, not in opposition to it. Thus, standards that address critical thinking, creative thinking, and problem solving are also highlighted as they interact with the development of the specified affective skills.

Standard 1: Learning and Development

Description: Educators, recognizing the learning and developmental differences of students with gifts and talents, promote ongoing self-understanding, awareness of their needs, and cognitive and affective growth of these students in school, home, and community settings to ensure specific student outcomes.

| Total Indicators for Standard 1 ||
Student Outcomes	Evidence-Based Practices
1.1. Self-Understanding. Students with gifts and talents demonstrate self-knowledge with respect to their interests, strengths, identities, and needs in socioemotional development and in intellectual, academic, creative, leadership, and artistic domains.	1.1.1. Educators engage students with gifts and talents in **identifying interests, strengths, and gifts.**
	1.1.2. Educators assist students with gifts and talents in developing identities supportive of achievement.
1.2. Self-Understanding. Students with gifts and talents possess a developmentally appropriate understanding of how they learn and grow; they recognize the influences of their beliefs, traditions, and values on their learning and behavior. *1.3. Self-Understanding.* Students with gifts and talents demonstrate understanding of and respect for similarities and differences between themselves and their peer group and others in the general population.	**1.2.1. Educators develop activities that match each student's developmental level and culture-based learning needs.**
1.4. Awareness of Needs. Students with gifts and talents access resources from the community to support cognitive and affective needs, including social interactions with others having similar interests and abilities or experiences, including same-age peers and mentors or experts and support students with gifts and talents' needs.	1.3.1. Educators provide a variety of research-based grouping practices for students with gifts and talents that allow them to interact with individuals of various gifts, talents, abilities, and strengths.
1.8. Cognitive and Affective Growth. Students with gifts and talents identify future career goals that match their talents and abilities and resources needed to meet those goals (e.g., higher education opportunities, mentors, financial support).	**1.3.2. Educators model respect for individuals with diverse abilities, strengths, and goals.**

Total Indicators for Standard 1, continued.	
Student Outcomes, continued.	Evidence-Based Practices, continued.
1.4. Awareness of Needs. Students with gifts and talents access resources from the community to support cognitive and affective needs, including social interactions with others having similar interests and abilities or experiences, including same-age peers and mentors or experts.	1.4.1. Educators **provide role models** (e.g., through mentors, bibliotherapy) for students with gifts and talents that match their abilities and interests.
1.5. Awareness of Needs. Students' families and communities understand similarities and differences with respect to the development and characteristics of advanced and typical learners and support students with gifts and talents' needs.	
1.6. Cognitive and Affective Growth. Students with gifts and talents benefit from meaningful and challenging learning activities addressing their unique characteristics and needs.	**1.6.1. Educators design interventions for students to develop cognitive and affective growth that is based on research of effective practices.**
	1.6.2. Educators develop specialized intervention services for students with gifts and talents who are underachieving and are now learning and developing their talents.
1.7. Cognitive and Affective Growth. Students with gifts and talents recognize their preferred approaches to learning and expand their repertoire.	
1.8. Cognitive and Affective Growth. Students with gifts and talents identify future career goals that match their talents and abilities and resources needed to meet those goals (e.g., higher education opportunities, mentors, financial support).	**1.8.1. Educators provide students with college and career guidance that is consistent with their strengths.**
	1.8.2. Teachers and counselors implement a curriculum scope and sequence that contains personal/social awareness and adjustment, academic planning, and vocational and career awareness.

Standard 3: Curriculum Planning and Instruction

Description: Educators apply the theory and research-based models of curriculum and instruction related to students with gifts and talents and respond to their needs by planning, selecting, adapting, and creating culturally relevant curriculum and by using a repertoire of evidence-based instructional strategies to ensure specific student outcomes.

Total Indicators for Standard 3	
Student Outcomes	Evidence-Based Practices
3.1. *Curriculum Planning.* Students with gifts and talents demonstrate growth commensurate with aptitude during the school year.	**3.1.1. Educators use local, state, and national standards to align and expand curriculum and instructional plans.**
	3.1.4. Educators design differentiated curricula that incorporate advanced, conceptually challenging, in-depth, distinctive, and complex content for students with gifts and talents.
	3.1.5. Educators use a balanced assessment system, including pre-assessment and formative assessment, to identify students' needs, develop differentiated education plans, and adjust plans based on continual progress monitoring.
	3.1.6. Educators use pre-assessments and pace instruction based on the learning rates of students with gifts and talents and accelerate and compact learning as appropriate.
3.2. *Talent Development.* Students with gifts and talents become more competent in multiple talent areas and across dimensions of learning.	**3.2.1. Educators design curricula in cognitive, affective, aesthetic, social, and leadership domains that are challenging and effective for students with gifts and talents.**
	3.2.2. Educators use metacognitive models to meet the needs of students with gifts and talents.
3.3. *Talent Development.* Students with gifts and talents develop their abilities in their domain of talent and/or area of interest.	**3.3.1. Educators select, adapt, and use a repertoire of instructional strategies and materials that differentiate for students with gifts and talents and that respond to diversity.**
	3.3.2. Educators use school and community resources that support differentiation.
	3.3.3. Educators provide opportunities for students with gifts and talents to explore, develop, or research their areas of interest and/or talent.

Total Indicators for Standard 3, continued.	
Student Outcomes, continued.	Evidence-Based Practices, continued.
3.4. *Instructional Strategies.* Students with gifts and talents become independent investigators.	**3.4.1. Educators use critical-thinking strategies to meet the needs of students with gifts and talents.**
	3.4.2. Educators use creative-thinking strategies to meet the needs of students with gifts and talents.
	3.4.3. Educators use problem-solving model strategies to meet the needs of students with gifts and talents.
	3.4.4. Educators use inquiry models to meet the needs of students with gifts and talents.
3.5. *Culturally Relevant Curriculum.* Students with gifts and talents develop knowledge and skills for living and being productive in a multicultural, diverse, and global society.	**3.5.1. Educators develop and use challenging, culturally responsive curriculum to engage all students with gifts and talents.**
	3.5.2. Educators integrate career exploration experiences into learning opportunities for students with gifts and talents (e.g., biography study or speakers).
	3.5.3. Educators use curriculum for deep explorations of cultures, languages, and social issues related to diversity.
3.6. *Resources.* Students with gifts and talents benefit from gifted education programming that provides a variety of high quality resources and materials.	3.6.1. Teachers and administrators demonstrate familiarity with sources for high quality resources and materials that are appropriate for learners with gifts and talents.

Standard 4: Learning Environments

Description: Learning environments foster personal and social responsibility, multicultural competence, and interpersonal and technical communication skills for leadership in the 21st century to ensure specific student outcomes.

Total Indicators for Standard 4	
Student Outcomes	Evidence-Based Practices
4.1. *Personal Competence.* Students with gifts and talents demonstrate growth in personal competence and dispositions for exceptional academic and creative productivity. These include self-awareness, self-advocacy, self-efficacy, confidence, motivation, resilience, independence, curiosity, and risk taking.	**4.1.1. Educators maintain high expectations for all students with gifts and talents as evidenced in meaningful and challenging activities.**
	4.1.2. Educators provide opportunities for self-exploration, development and pursuit of interests, and development of identities supportive of achievement (e.g., through mentors and role models).
	4.1.3. Educators create environments that support trust among diverse learners.
	4.1.4. Educators provide feedback that focuses on effort, on evidence of potential to meet high standards, and on mistakes as learning opportunities.
	4.1.5. Educators provide examples of positive coping skills and opportunities to apply them.
4.2. *Social Competence.* Students with gifts and talents develop social competence manifested in positive peer relationships and social interactions.	4.2.1. Educators understand the needs of students with gifts and talents for both solitude and social interaction.
	4.2.2. Educators provide opportunities for interaction with intellectual and artistic/creative peers as well as with chronological-age peers.
	4.2.3. Educators assess and provide instruction on social skills needed for school, community, and the world of work.
4.3. *Leadership.* Students with gifts and talents demonstrate personal and social responsibility and leadership skills.	4.3.1 Educators establish a safe and welcoming climate for addressing social issues and developing personal responsibility.
	4.3.2. Educators provide environments for developing many forms of leadership and leadership skills.

Total Indicators for Standard 4, continued.	
Student Outcomes, continued.	Evidence-Based Practices, continued.
4.4. *Cultural Competence*. Students with gifts and talents value their own and others' language, heritage, and circumstance. They possess skills in communicating, teaming, and collaborating with diverse individuals and across diverse groups.[1] They use positive strategies to address social issues, including discrimination and stereotyping.	**4.4.1. Educators model appreciation for and sensitivity to students' diverse backgrounds and languages.**
	4.4.2. Educators censure discriminatory language and behavior and model appropriate strategies.
	4.4.3. Educators provide structured opportunities to collaborate with diverse peers on a common goal.
4.5. *Communication Competence*. Students with gifts and talents develop competence in interpersonal and technical communication skills. They demonstrate advanced oral and written skills, balanced biliteracy or multiliteracy, and creative expression. They display fluency with technologies that support effective communication.	**4.5.1. Educators provide opportunities for advanced development and maintenance of first and second language(s).**
	4.5.2. Educators provide resources to enhance oral, written, and artistic forms of communication, recognizing students' cultural context.
	4.5.3. Educators ensure access to advanced communication tools, including assistive technologies, and use of these tools for expressing higher-level thinking and creative productivity.